T0270894

Sustainable Development
Goals and Integrated Reporting

Cristiano Busco - Fabrizio Granà - Maria Federica Izzo

Sustainable Development Goals and Integrated Reporting

First published 2018
by Routledge
2 Park Square, Milton Park, Abingdon, Oxon OX14 4RN

and by Routledge
52 Vanderbilt Avenue, New York, NY 10017

First issued in paperback 2020

Routledge is an imprint of the Taylor & Francis Group, an informa business

and by G. Giappichelli Editore
Via Po 21, Torino – Italia

British Library Cataloguing-in-Publication Data
A catalogue record for this book is available from the British Library

ISBN 13: 978-0-367-58318-7 (pbk)
ISBN 13: 978-1-138-31337-8 (hbk)

Typeset in Simoncini Garamond
by G. Giappichelli Editore, Turin, Italy

The manuscript has been subjected to the double blind peer review process prior to publication.

TABLE OF CONTENTS

LIST OF TABLES AND FIGURES

LIST OF AUTHORS

Cristiano Busco, Ph.D., is professor of Accounting and Integrated Reporting at Roehampton University, in London and LUISS Guido Carli University, Rome, Italy. Cristiano has earned a PhD (accounting) at University of Manchester, UK, and has hold teaching and research positions within US (University of Southern California, LA, and Babson College, Boston), UK (Manchester Business School), Irish (National University of Ireland, Galway) and Italian universities (University of Siena).

Cristiano research interests are in the field of management accounting, performance measurement, as well as integrated thinking and reporting. He published in peer-reviewed journals such as Contemporary Accounting Research, Management Accounting Research, Journal of Management and Governance, Qualitative Research in Accounting and Management, Journal of Accounting and Change, and Business Horizons as well as in professional journals such as the Journal of Corporate Accounting and Finance, Strategic Finance and, Financial Management.

Fabrizio Granà, Ph.D., is Post Doc at LUISS Guido Carli University, Rome (Italy). Fabrizio has earned a PhD (accounting) at National University of Ireland Galway, IE.

His research interests focus on the role of accounting and Reporting practices for sustainable development. In particular, he focuses on integrated thinking and integrated management.

Previously, Fabrizio has been research assistant at Roehampton University, in London (UK), and visiting researcher at the University of Edinburgh Business School, Edinburgh (UK). In the field of Integrated Thinking and Reporting, Fabrizio has collaborated on some research project with UniCredit and Eni.

Maria Federica Izzo, Ph.D., is Lecturer at LUISS Guido Carli University, Rome, Italy, where she teaches Advanced Management Accounting and Business Administration.

Previously she has been Assistant Professor at LUISS Guido Carli; visiting scholar at Jones Graduate School of Management, Rice University, Houston and research assistant at London Business School.

Maria Federica research interests are in the field of performance measurement, financial accounting as well as sustainable development. On the sustainability issues, Maria Federica has collaborated with listed companies as, among the others, AS Roma S.p.A. and Enel S.p.a.

Chapter 1

MAKE SUSTAINABLE DEVELOPMENT GOALS HAPPEN THROUGH INTEGRATED THINKING: AN INTRODUCTION

by *Cristiano Busco*

SUMMARY: 1.1. Introduction. – 1.2. The discourse on sustainable development and the SDGs. – 1.3. Achieving the SDGs through Integrated Thinking. – 1.4. PepsiCo: governing sustainability through Performance with Purpose. – 1.5. How Eni pursues the SDGs. – 1.6. Make SDGs happen through Integrated Thinking: what role for the Finance function and for Accounting and Reporting practices? – 1.7. References.

1.1. Introduction

Our planet faces massive global economic, social, and environmental challenges – we know that very well. We also know that the promise of globalisation is being increasingly endangered by political uncertainty and, eventually, by a rising tide of nationalism and protectionism recently emerged across the globe. To deal with these major challenges and uncertainties, in September 2015 Governments worldwide have agreed on seventeen Sustainable Development Goals (SDGs). Promoted by the United Nations, the SDGs define global priorities and aspirations for 2030, and they rely on the critical role of business organizations in delivering on the promise of sustainable and inclusive development (see Scheyren *et al.*, 2016; Bebbington and Unerman, 2017).

Making SDGs happen will be the challenge of the years ahead. Several business organizations across the globe have started this journey by identifying and executing sustainable strategies as key drivers of their purpose, visions and business models. While, on the one hand the SDGs present an opportunity for business-led solutions and technologies to be developed, on the other hand they offer an overarching framework to shape, steer, measure and report the value created through business objectives, initiatives, and performance. Measuring and reporting business models for long term value creation shall enable organizations to contribute to the SDGs while capitalizing on a range of benefits such as identifying future business opportunities, strengthening stakeholder engagement, and communicating whom they can share the value created with.

As contemporary organizations familiarise with the SDGs' discourse and agenda, it must be acknowledged that they are currently operating in a very complex world, characterised by a multitude of internal and external drivers, interdependencies and trade-offs, that influence the process of decision making, the promises that these decisions entail, and the expectations of a variety of demanding stakeholders. For these reasons, organization leaders are increasingly required to navigate through these challenges by implementing a comprehensive and inclusive approach to planning, measurement, and reporting. Among other approaches to accounting and reporting, Integrated Reporting (IR) seem to represent a promising approach to disclose corporates journey towards the SDGs (Adams, 2017).

Whether presented as a possible rational choice for facing existing challenges (see, among recent contributions, Adams and Simnett, 2011; Adams, 2015; Serafeim, 2015; Barth *et al.*, 2017), as a ceremonial response to the increasing pressures of markets and society (Higgins *et al.*, 2014; van Bommel, 2014), or as a temporary fad and fashion (Thomson, 2015; Flower, 2015; de Villiers and Sharma, 2017), Integrated Reporting (IR) has rapidly gained considerable prominence as one of the main management and accounting innovations of the recent decade (de Villiers *et al.*, 2014; Simnett and Huggins, 2015; Dumay *et al.*, 2016). Grounded in a process labelled – by its advocators – as integrated thinking, since 2011 IR has been promoted by the IIRC (International Integrated Reporting Council) for the resulting periodic and concise integrated report on how an organization's strategy, governance, performance, and prospects lead to the creation of sustainable value in the short, medium, and long term.[1] In December 2013, after years in which a group of early adopters developed the concept of IR as part of their reporting practices, the IIRC released a Framework to serve as a guide for the voluntary adoption of this novel form of corporate reporting.

What are the SDGs? Where do they come from? Are companies ready to engage with them? How? What is the possible role of accountants, and finance leaders more in general, in this space? The purpose of this chapter is to introduce these themes, which will then be addressed more in detail in the rest of the book. In particular, after having introduced the SDGs (section 1.2), we will discuss the possible role of Integrated Thinking in moving organizations towards the SDGs' agenda (1.3). Then, we will rely on the early examples of PepsiCo (1.4) and Eni (1.5) to discuss how the sustaina-

---

[1] See IIRC (2013), The International <IR> Framework – http://www.theiirc.org/international-ir-framework/.

ble strategy in place are linked to the SDGs within corporate reports. Finally, this introductory chapter ends with some reflections concerning the role of the finance function as well as accounting and reporting practices in steering the organizations towards the achievement of the SDGs.

1.2. The discourse on sustainable development and the SDGs

Over the past thirty years or so, world leaders, supranational organizations, national governments as well as private and public organizations have progressively embraced sustainability as the cornerstone of the promissory discourse in their search for development and long-term growth. Conceptualised as the means to achieve sustainability, sustainable development has been defined in 1987 by the United Nation Brundtland report as "development that meets the needs of the present without compromising the ability of future generations to meet their own needs".

In the years following the release of the Brundtland Report, multiple institutions and international bodies have further attempted to identify the core elements of the sustainable development discourse. With the intention to address the numerous issues broadly referred to as the domain of sustainable development (such as water emergency, health, climate change, pollution, social inequalities, access to energy, extreme poverty, and hunger), several major events and initiatives have taken place globally (see Bebbington, 2001, for a review). For example, at the Johannesburg World Summit in 2002, sustainable development was defined as embracing not only environmental aspects, but also social inclusion and economic development.

In 2012, the concept of sustainable development was further refined by the United Nations (see UN, The Future we want, 2012), and extended in 2013 by the United Nation Sustainable Development Solution Network (UNSDSN), with the inclusion of good governance as a fourth pillar. In parallel, public, private and non-governmental organizations have been directly involved in the attempt to ensure more coordinated efforts regarding the 'sustainability agenda' (see, e.g., the UN General Assembly resolution in 2010). This process has been consolidated in 2015 when the General Assembly of the United Nations adopted the 2030 Agenda for Sustainable Development, accompanied by a list of Sustainable Development Goals (SDGs – namely, 17 objectives and 169 targets), which will have to be achieved by all countries of the world by 2030 (see Kumar et al, 2017; Bebbington and Unerman, 2017).

In terms of goals to be achieved, earlier, the twenty-first century started with a set of development goals, known as Millennium Development Goals (MDGs). Designed for global action, between 2000 and 2015 the MDGs provided an important development framework and achieved success in several areas such as reducing poverty and improving health and education in developing countries. Gaining from the experience of MDGs, the UN decided to expand the goals to make them much wider, encompassing both developed and developing countries, and expanding the challenges that must be addressed embracing a wide range of inter-connected topics across the economic, social, and environmental dimensions of sustainable development.

This led to the identification and release of the SDGs, which were born out of what is arguably the most inclusive process in the history of the United Nations, reflecting substantive input from all sectors of society and all parts of the world (Sachs, 2012). The goals are universally applicable in developing and developed countries alike. Governments are expected to translate them into national action plans, policies, and initiatives, reflecting the different realities and capacities their countries possess. Differently from the MDGs, the SDGs are designed to rally a wide range of organizations, and shape priorities and aspirations for sustainable development efforts around a common framework. Most importantly, the SDGs recognize the key role that business can and must play in achieving them.

As summarised in Exhibit 1, the SDGs encompass (1) to end poverty in all its forms everywhere; (2) to end hunger, achieve food security, improve nutrition, and promote sustainable agriculture; (3) to ensure healthy lives and promote well-being for all; (4) to ensure inclusive and quality education for all; (5) to achieve gender equality and empower all women; (6) to ensure access to water and sanitation for all; (7) to ensure access to affordable, reliable and sustainable energy for all; (8) to promote inclusive and sustainable economic growth, employment and decent work for all; (9) to build resilient infrastructure, promote sustainable industrialization and foster innovation; (10) to reduce inequality within and among countries; (11) to make cities inclusive, safe, resilient and sustainable; (12) to ensure sustainable consumption and production patterns; (13) to combat climate change; (14) to conserve and sustainably use the oceans, seas and marine resources; (15) to sustainably manage forests, combat desertification, halt land degradation, and halt biodiversity loss; (16) to promote inclusive societies; and (17) Strengthen the means of implementation and revitalize the global partnership for sustainable development.

Exhibit 1.1. The 17 Sustainable Development Goals.

1.3. Achieving the SDGs through Integrated Thinking

Attempting to achieve the SDGs isn't just a show of governmental and so-cietal goodwill – it's also a strategy increasingly made by proactive, sustainable organizations. Making SDG alignment part of their strategies and business models can help companies generate new revenue, increase supply chain resilience, recruit and retain talent, spawn investor interest, and assure license to operate. Such business organizations want to achieve the same ends as any other company by driving revenue growth, creating value, and accelerating business expansion. Critically, however, contributing to the SDGs through inclusive business models helps these organizations reinforce their awareness regarding the multiple and heterogeneous resources they use as well as the impact of the company's activities on stakeholders. Notably, this attempt seems to call for an integrated approach to planning, measurement and reporting.

Whether large or small, private or public, for-profit or non-profit, every year organizations invest a vast amount of resources, time and energy as their intertwined cycles of planning, measurement and reporting unfold recursively in practice. Designed and prepared to fulfil the expectations of external and internal stakeholders, corporate reports are positioned at the final stage of these cycles as they highlight and summarise the processes of strategic planning, operations management and performance measurement that are in place. Within this context, and in the attempt to offer an account of the ongoing search for competitiveness and sustainable growth featuring contemporary organizations, annual reports are nowadays expected to convey insightful information beyond the traditional key financial data. Arguably, these reports are increasingly considered to be worthwhile reading due to their ability to inform readers about the way in which the organization's purpose and inclusive business model align with market opportunities and sustainable performance.

The concepts, elements and principles that characterize the way in which organizations plan, measure, and report their annual performance, as well as the relevance of corporate reporting, have all been questioned lately regarding a number of aspects, ranging from the supposed compliance-driven content they provide to the failure of offering forward-looking information about company strategy, performance, and risk. This perception has worsened in the aftermath of the recent financial crisis and corporate scandals, in which several commentators and analysts have firmly portrayed the global economic system as broken and have viewed organizations as being one of the major causes of social, environmental, and economic problems. This has led many experts, as well as public opinion, to criticise these fundamental documents as gradually becoming less fit for the purpose and often failing to shed light on strategy execution as well as on the extensive variety of intangible and natural resources used within an organization's processes of value creation.

Perhaps a metaphor would be useful to fully illustrate the heart of the matter. Take, for example, informative books such as a recipe book. On one hand, one may wonder whether anyone would ever be interested in reading a cookbook that talks about a variety of dishes without including listings of all the necessary ingredients.

On the other hand, would anybody ever delve into a cookbook that simply lists the ingredients of the recipes without offering any sort of cooking instructions? Well, if the answer to these questions is "no", and the reader is interested in knowing more about the concepts, stories and practices through which a number of contemporary organizations are currently dealing with the increasing pressure to align the organization's purpose and inclusive business model with market opportunities and sustainable performance(s), then the following pages in the book should be worth reading. Ultimately, if organizations intend to communicate their – more or less inclusive – recipe for value creation to their stakeholders, they need to understand it first and then make sure this awareness is reflected in the innovative forms of accounting and reporting for stakeholders that analysts and commentators are calling for.

Positioned at the centre of this debate, Integrated Reporting (IR) has been portrayed by an emerging body of professional and academic literature as in the transition phase from promising concept to powerful practice. Developed and promoted by the IIRC (International Integrated Reporting Council), IR is presented by its proponents as a process founded on Integrated Thinking, which results in a periodic and concise integrated report about how an organization's strategy, governance, performance and prospects lead to the creation of sustainable value in the short, medium and long term. Integrated Thinking is a term that refers to the conditions and processes that are conducive to an inclusive process of decision making, management and reporting, based on the connectivity and interdependencies between a range of factors that affect an organization's ability to create value over time.

The Framework released by the IIRC in December 2013 suggests that the fundamental concepts of Integrated Thinking and Reporting are represented by the capitals that an organization uses and affects, as well as the process of creating value over time. This value is embodied in the capitals – also referred to as resources and relationships. As illustrated in the Framework, organizations depend on six different types of capitals, which are stores of value that, in one form or another, become inputs to an organization's business model. They are: financial, manufactured, intellectual, human, social and relationship, and natural. The Framework doesn't require organizations to adopt the capitals, so they should be rather used as a benchmark to ensure an organization doesn't overlook a capital that it uses or affects.

Value is created or destroyed through the capitals within a company's business model, which represents the chosen system of inputs, business activities, outputs, and outcomes that aims to create value over the short, medium, and long term. Since these capitals and their value change over time as they are increased, decreased, or transformed through the activities and outputs of the organization, it's also important to understand how the outputs affect outcome. Whether the IIRC, and the Integrated Reporting movement at large, will succeed in making IR "the one" long-lasting solution addressing the rising concerns about accounting for stakeholders, (including shareholders), is hard to say. However, the stories, challenges and opportunities that characterize this innovative journey embraced by a number of organizations seem to be definitely worth taking a look, at as it aligned with the efforts of contributing to the achievement of the SDGs.

As suggested above, the integration between sustainability initiatives and business goals is progressively happening in practice. An increasing number of organizations are aligning their inclusive corporate purpose with the execution of sustainable strategies and the SDGs. While the evidence from the field will be addressed in detail in the following chapters, next, within this introductory chapter, we briefly shed light on the early experiences of PepsiCo and Eni to illustrate how this process took place in two fundamental industries such as Food and Beverage, and Energy. Ultimately, these examples demonstrate how businesses' growth and socioeconomic development can thrive together.

1.4. PepsiCo: governing sustainability through Performance with Purpose

PepsiCo's attention toward sustainable development received a boost in 2006 when the company launched its "Performance with Purpose" strategy, PepsiCo's vision to deliver top-tier financial performance over the long term by integrating sustainability into business strategy (this section is derived from the PepsiCo 2015 Global Reporting Initiative (GRI) Report and Performance with Purpose 2015 Agenda www.pepsico.com/sustainability/Sustainability-Reporting).

As shown in its 2015 Global Reporting Initiative Report and Performance with Purpose 2015 Agenda, PepsiCo has centered Performance with Purpose work on Products (human sustainability), Planet (environmental sustainability), and People (talent sustainability) – See Exhibit 1.2. More recently, the company began closely mapping its Performance with Purpose plans to the SDGs.

PepsiCo put in place a strong sustainability governance as the foundation for delivering on the Performance with Purpose vision. Sustainability topics are integrated into, not separate from, the core business. PepsiCo's Board considers sustainability issues an integral part of its business oversight. For example, the Board addresses sustainability issues in its oversight of focus areas such as capital allocation, supply chain management, talent retention, and portfolio innovation.

In 2015, after discussions with external stakeholders, the Board clarified its role with respect to sustainability by amending the company's Corporate Governance Guidelines to add "sustainability" to the key aspects of PepsiCo's business over which the Board has oversight responsibilities. In addition to full Board oversight of sustainability, the Board's Nominating and Corporate Governance Committee was charged with annually reviewing

PepsiCo's key public policy issues, including its sustainability initiatives, and its engagement in the public policy process. PepsiCo's sustainability governance structure reaches across the organization and focuses on three key areas whose successful development depends on management accounting and reporting practices:

1. Governance and Decision Making. Accountabilities are assigned to individuals or teams to set strategy, prioritize activities, identify gaps, and facilitate decision making needed to advance the sustainability agenda.

2. Tracking and Reporting Metrics (specific, measurable, time-bound targets). Where appropriate, metrics are defined and standardized for tracking progress against Performance with Purpose pillars. Additionally, reporting obligations are defined, and protocols are put in place to ensure compliance and data verification.

3. Facilitating Business Integration. Each pillar has a sustainability agenda and has developed scorecards, checklists, and timelines focused specifically on measuring PepsiCo progress against its current targets.

Exhibit 1.2. Performance with Purpose at PepsiCo.

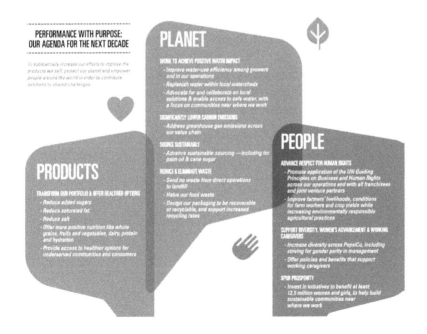

Source: PepsiCo GRI 2015 Report, p. 5.

Recently, PepsiCo reviewed the sustainability governance structure to identify opportunities to strengthen the integration of Performance with Purpose into its business agenda and processes. Going forward, the Pepsi-Co Executive Committee will assume direct oversight of the sustainability agenda, make strategic decisions, and champion performance management. Theme leads, empowered by the Executive Committee, will be appointed as subject matter experts to create and oversee global roadmap development and ensure business alignment to deliver on the goals. They are selected for their deep knowledge of the goals they are directing, and they work with teams composed of representatives from key functions across all geographic sectors (sector leads). Theme leads will align their agendas with the sector leads, who will be on point to ensure successful implementation of processes across businesses. Theme leads will be supported by the Sustainability Office, which will be responsible for driving the strategic framework and performance tracking.

Performance with Purpose allows PepsiCo to make valuable contributions to the SDGs. By focusing on creating and sustaining jobs, stimulating economic growth, transforming the product portfolio, protecting the planet, and enhancing the lives of people around the world, the company believes that impactful contributions to the SDGs will be made through its own business and its value chain – see Exhibit 1.3. Additionally, the PepsiCo Foundation, which aligns with PepsiCo's Performance with Purpose strategy and the SDGs, aims to provide opportunities for improved health, environmental conservation, and education in underserved regions through sustainable development partnerships and programs. All these are measures of PepsiCo's success.

Exhibit 1.3. Aligning Performance with Purpose to the SDGs.

CONTRIBUTING TO THE UN SUSTAINABLE DEVELOPMENT GOALS

PepsiCo's Performance with Purpose agenda allows us to make valuable contributions to goals shared by the global community. The SDGs call for worldwide action among governments, business and civil society to end hunger, protect the planet and enrich the lives of people around the world.

	PRODUCTS GOALS	PLANET GOALS	PEOPLE GOALS
1. NO POVERTY			✓
2. ZERO HUNGER	✓	✓	✓
3. GOOD HEALTH AND WELLBEING	✓	✓	✓
4. QUALITY EDUCATION			✓
5. GENDER EQUALITY			✓
6. CLEAN WATER AND SANITATION		✓	✓
7. AFFORDABLE AND CLEAN ENERGY		✓	
8. DECENT WORK AND ECONOMIC GROWTH			✓
9. INDUSTRY, INNOVATION AND INFRASTRUCTURE	✓	✓	
10. REDUCED INEQUALITIES			✓
11. SUSTAINABLE CITIES AND COMMUNITIES		✓	✓
12. RESPONSIBLE CONSUMPTION AND PRODUCTION	✓	✓	
13. CLIMATE ACTION		✓	
14. LIFE BELOW WATER		✓	
15. LIFE ON LAND		✓	✓
16. PEACE, JUSTICE AND STRONG INSTITUTIONS			✓
17. PARTNERSHIPS FOR THE GOALS	✓	✓	✓

Source: PepsiCo GRI 2015 Report, p. 5.

Like PepsiCo, the Italian energy giant Eni has invested time and resources in making sure that business strategies embody sustainability initiatives at their very core. For these reasons, over the last 10 years Eni has supported such a massive process of integration by innovating its management and accounting practices (see Busco *et al.*, 2013; 2014). Now alignment with the SDGs seems a natural step in a process that's rooted in making sustainability happen through inclusive strategies and business models.

1.5. How Eni pursues the SDGs

Labelled as *Eni for 2016*, the company's Sustainability Report declares up-front how the 17 SDGs are used as a guide for project development over the long term (www.eni.com/en_IT/home.page). The report suggests how the private sector can, and must, play a crucial role as the engine of sustain-able development over the long term, balancing global business and finan-cial goals and local socio-economic growth. This has led Eni to measure it-self against the SDGs and reinforce the involvement in devising concrete solutions to move toward SDG achievement.

As a major operator in the energy field, Eni has two great challenges: maximizing access to energy and combatting climate change. To overcome these important challenges, Eni has defined a long-term integrated strategy to reconcile financial stability with social and environmental sustainability to create long-term value for all the stakeholders. To implement these stra-tegic guidelines, Eni is leveraging three key levers (see Exhibit 1.4):

– A well-defined path to decarbonization;
– An operating model that reduces risks as well as environmental and social impacts; and
– A model with the hosting countries based on long-lasting partnership and cooperation.

First, Eni's commitment in promoting a well-defined path to decarboni-zation lies mainly in reducing its activities' emissions, developing renewable energies, and guaranteeing access to energy. With its plan to reduce green-house gas emissions, in 2016 Eni continued to reduce the emissions intensi-ty index by 9% and is committed to continue to do so in order to reach the 43% reduction goal in 2025. The company will also continue to increase natural gas production, the bridge toward a low-carbon future, and to de-velop projects to install a capacity of 463 megawatts from renewables by 2020.

Exhibit 1.4. Eni's Strategic Guidelines as linked to the SDGs.

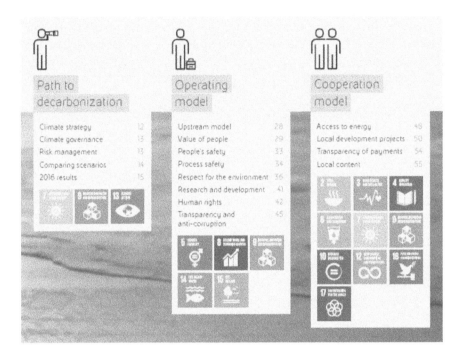

Source: Eni for 2016, Contents page.

Second, to make access to new energy resources more efficient and minimize risks throughout the whole production cycle, Eni plans to conduct its business using an operating model of excellence aimed at safeguarding people and assets, respecting the environment, and engaging in research and development. Thanks to this model, over the last three years the company has registered Total Recordable Injury Rate (TRIR) values for both employees and contractors that were significantly lower than the peer average. In 2016, Eni reduced the TRIR by 20.8% compared with 2015, with the aim to reach zero injuries as the company continues investing in training to spread its safety-first culture.

Third, Eni's cooperation model has been finalized to support local development, to minimize socioeconomic gaps, and to engage all the stakeholders. In this way, the company's method of working aims at filling the gaps of local development and developing local resources for local growth. In the territories where Eni is present, the company doesn't simply invest in the oil and gas production for export but mostly for the inland market while also investing in sectors that are distant from its own business, such as power stations to provide regional access to energy, promote local entre-preneurship, economic diversification, access to drinking water, and community health and education. For example, in Congo and Nigeria the company has invested $2 billion, respectively, providing about 60% and 20% of the electricity of these two countries. This model soon will be repeated in Angola and Ghana.

Exhibit 1.5. Integrated Performance Dashboard.

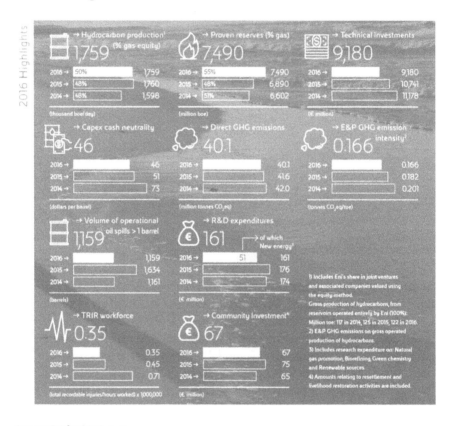

Source: Eni for 2016, p. 4.

Eni's contributions to the SDGs through the execution of inclusive business and holistic projects development build on a new way to look at performance measurement and reporting. With the intention of better understanding, communicating, and executing its business model and the strategy identified by the Board, over the last five years Eni has innovated its management and accounting systems by turning to integrated thinking and reporting. Championed by the vice president for sustainability and subsequently fully embraced by the Finance organization, the adoption of this emerging practice was carried out by a workgroup composed of managers from Finance, Sustainability, External Relations, Corporate Governance, and Integrated Risk Management. The main goal was to offer a comprehensive view of the process of value creation by monitoring and connecting those key financial and pre-financial performance(s) essential to sustain the execution of sustainable strategies (See Exhibit 1.5 for an illustration of these integrated dashboards).

Eni's approach to integrated thinking and reporting departed from a deeper understanding of the financial and operating objectives featuring the organization's strategic plan and linked them with the resources used, the initiatives implemented, and the interdependences among the various drivers at work. The purpose was to highlight the way in which initiatives of sustainability contributed to achieving the strategic targets of the company. An interesting example is offered by upstream division, where financial returns and exploration success were linked to operational excellence and innovation.

Eni's performance measurement and reporting systems enable the company to monitor and measure the results achieved in the upstream area by applying the Dual Exploration Model. If this model's primary goal was to replace the existing reserves and, therefore, sustain organic production growth in the future through exploration, it makes it possible to immediately exploit certain discoveries and to generate cash flow through the sale of minority interests in some assets. This support in cash flow generated without compromising the goal of organically replacing the reserves at the same time reduces its financial exposure with regard to investments in the main projects.

Eni's holistic, integrated approach to measurement and reporting implemented by Eni permitted the company to highlight and value the key drivers of such a distinctive exploration strategy, which is based on a medium- to long-term vision; a focus on time to market; a governance and management of exploration processes; a professional development of Eni's workforce; an ability to protect, disseminate, and renew know-how; a constant focus on the opportunities provided by technological innovation; and, finally, rigorous attention to Health, Safety, and Environmental (HSE) aspects. From a measurement and reporting point of view, Eni decided to capture the effects of specific actions and initiatives taken in the upstream business and their impact on business objectives and risks in a cause-effect map showing a comprehensive connectivity of performance(s) (see Exhibit 1.6).

Exhibit 1.6. Connectivity of Performances Map.

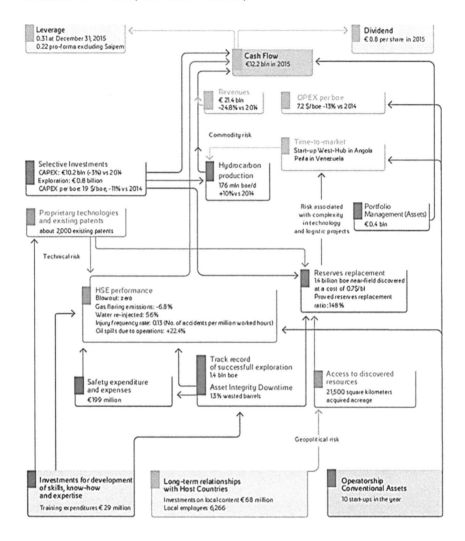

Source: Eni Annual Integrated Report 2015, p. 20.

1.6. Make SDGs happen through Integrated Thinking: what role for the Finance function and for Accounting and Reporting practices?

Integrated Thinking is about connecting performance with purpose. It involves identifying, executing, and monitoring business decisions and strategies for long-term value creation. Integrated Thinking builds on the need to reconcile competitiveness and sustainable growth within the context of inclusive business models in order to take advantage of the opportunities and face the challenges of the market. For these reasons, as we have seen in the case of PepsiCo and Eni illustrated above, Integrated Thinking (and Reporting) can possibly contribute to aligning business organizations with the SDGs.

Nowadays most business organizations strive to balance competitiveness and sustainable growth by implementing programs and initiatives of sustainability intending to achieve specific targets in terms of governance, social, and environmental impact. But a mishmash of sustainability tactics does not guarantee the achievement of sustainable performance(s), which instead requires an integrated approach to the planning, management and reporting, that must take into consideration how the interests and the contributions of a series of heterogeneous stakeholders are linked into the models for long-term value creation.

Within this context, accounting and reporting offer tools and engagement platforms that are able to go beyond the mere representation of the initiatives of sustainability through a set of ad hoc targets and key performance indicators, to include processes of mediation among the different stakeholders who are involved. In this space, accountants, and finance experts in general, lead the search for sustainable performance by suggesting pragmatic solutions that are able to monitor and communicate ways in which such an inclusive business purpose may be converted into added value for a multitude of stakeholders – also in light of the SDGs. Finance experts often takes a centre stage in these situations, acting as both architects and orchestrators of an integrated process of thinking, measuring and reporting that mediates among multiple concerns, facilitates conversations, and fosters the generation of innovative solutions within contexts that are characterised by multiple backgrounds and points of view.

Whether recent critical academic and professional studies present Integrated Thinking and Reporting as a possible rational choice for facing existing challenges, a ceremonial response to the increasing pressures of markets and society, a temporary fad and fashion, this book acknowledges that this novel form of reporting has rapidly gained considerable prominence as one of the main management and accounting innovations of the recent decade. And this trend is due to continue – with several organizations adopting integrated thinking as a basis to foster internal processes of change. Our research and experience suggest that to make this happen effectively there is a need for internal sponsorship from a very high level: usually Board, CEO or CFO. Finance experts can play a very important role in these initiatives, as they manage processes to collect data, provide narratives, interpretation and analysis, and link with other functions.

Leading practices typically centre on the link between the Balanced Scorecard and Strategy Maps, presentation of the multiple "Capitals", and facilitation of engagement across multiple stakeholders. The main challenges concern identifying useful, reliable indicators, reporting them consistently and gaining buy-in from internal and external stakeholders. Later in the book we will highlight some recommendations to be considered by finance experts, accountants, and by all other organization leaders who intend to design and manage effective processes of Integrated Thinking to make sustainable strategies happen and contribute towards the achievement of the SGDs.

1.7. References

Adams, C. (2017), The Sustainable Development Goals, integrated thinking and the Integrated report, http://integratedreporting.org/resource/sdgs-integrated-thinking-and-the-integrated-report/. Accessed 8 December 2017.

Adams, C.A. (2015), "The international integrated reporting council: a call to action", *Critical Perspectives on Accounting*, Vol. 27, pp. 23-28.

Adams, S. and Simnett, R. (2011), "Integrated reporting: an opportunity for Australia's not-for-profit sector", *Australian Accounting Review*, Vol. 21 No. 3, pp. 292-301.

Barth, M.E., Cahan S.F., Chen, L., Venter, E.R. (2017), "The economic consequences associated with integrated report quality: Capital market and real effects", *Accounting, Organizations and Society*, Vol. 62, pp. 43-64.

Bebbington, J. (2001), "Sustainable development: a review of the international development, business and accounting literature", *Accounting Forum*, Vol. 25, No. 2, pp. 128-157.

Bebbington, J., Unerman, J., (2017), "Achieving the United Nations Sustainable Development Goals: an enabling role for accounting research", *Accounting, Auditing & Accountability Journal*, https://doi.org/10.1108/AAAJ-05-2017-2929.

Bommel, K. (2014), "Towards a legitimate compromise?: an exploration of Integrated Reporting in the Netherlands", *Accounting, Auditing & Accountability Journal*, Vol. 27 No. 7, pp. 1157-1189.

de Villiers, C. and Sharma, U. (2017), "A critical reflection on the future of financial, intellectual capital, sustainability and integrated reporting", *Critical Perspectives on Accounting*, http://dx.doi.org/10.1016/j.cpa.2017.05.003.

de Villiers, C., Rinaldi, L., Unerman, J. (2014), "Integrated Reporting: Insights, gaps and an agenda for future research", *Accounting, Auditing & Accountability Journal*, Vol. 27 No. 7, pp. 1042-1067.

Dumay, J., Bernardi, C., Guthrie, J., Demartini, P. (2016), "Integrated reporting: A structured literature review", *Accounting Forum*, Vol. 40 No. 2016, pp. 166-185.

Eni (2015), Annual Integrated Report 2015. https://www.eni.com/docs/en_IT/enicom/company/company-profile/Integrated-Annual-Report-2015.pdf. Accessed 8 December 2017.

Eni (2016), Eni for 2016. https://www.eni.com/docs/en_IT/enicom/ sustainability/EniFor-2016.pdf. Accessed 8 December 2017.

Flower, J. (2015), "The International Integrated Reporting Council: a story of failure", *Critical Perspectives on Accounting*. Vol. 27, pp. 1-17.

Higgins, C., Stubbs, W., Love, T. (2014), "Walking the talk(s): Organisational narratives of integrated reporting", *Accounting, Auditing & Accountability Journal*, Vol. 27 No. 7, pp. 1090-1119.

Kumar, P., Ahmed, F., Singh, R. and Sinha, P. (2017), "Determination of hierarchical relationships among sustainable development goals using interpretive structure modelling", *Environment, Development and Sustainability*. https://doi.org/10.1007/s10668-017-9981-1

PepsiCo (2015) GRI 2015 Report. http://www.pepsico.com/docs/album/sustainability-reporting/final_pep_2015_gri.pdf. Accessed 8 December 2017.

Sachs, J. (2012), "From Millennium Development Goals to Sustainable Development Goals", *The Lancet*, Vol. 379, pp. 2206-2211.

Scheyvens, R., Banks, G., and Hughes, E, (2016), "The Private Sector and the SDGs: The Need to Move Beyond 'Business as Usual'", *Sustainable Development*, Vol. 24, No. 6, pp. 371-382.

Serafeim, G. (2015), "Integrated Reporting and Investor Clientele", *Journal of Applied Corporate Finance*, Vol. 27 No. 2, pp. 34-51.

Simnett, R., Huggins, A.L. (2015), "Integrated reporting and assurance: where can research add value?", *Sustainability Accounting, Management and Policy Journal*, Vol. 6 No. 1, pp. 29-53.

Thomson, I. (2015), "But Does Sustainability need Capitalism or an Integrated Report a Commentary on 'The International Integrated Reporting Council: A Story of Failure' by Flower, J.", *Critical Perspectives on Accounting*, Vol. 27, pp. 18-22.

United Nation UN (2012), The Future We Want, https://sustainabledevelopment.un.org/content/documents/733FutureWeWant.pdf. Accessed 8 December 2017.

Chapter 2

PRACTICING INTEGRATED THINKING: TOWARDS A NEW ERA OF CORPORATE MANAGEMENT ACCOUNTING AND REPORTING

by *Fabrizio Granà*

SUMMARY: 2.1. Introduction. – 2.2. Towards the integration of financial and non-financial performance. – 2.3. Integrated Reporting and Integrated Thinking. – 2.3.1. Fundamental concepts. – 2.3.2. Guiding principles. – 2.3.3. Content elements. – 2.4. Integrated Thinking in practice: the case of UniCredit Group and SASOL South Africa. – 2.4.1. UniCredit Group. – 2.4.2. SASOL South Africa. – 2.5. Benefits and critics of Integrated Thinking and Reporting. – 2.6. Summary and conclusions. – 2.7. References.

2.1. Introduction

Contemporary organizations are required to balance competitiveness and sustainable growth by implementing programs and initiatives of sustainability with the aim of achieving specific targets in terms of governance, social, and environmental impact.

Organization leaders are increasingly asked to navigate through these challenges by implementing a comprehensive approach to planning, measurement and reporting. In particular, management accountants and finance experts lead the search for sustainable performance by suggesting pragmatic solutions that are able to monitor and communicate ways in which such an inclusive business purpose may be converted into added value for a multitude of stakeholders.

In this context, management accounting and reporting practices offer tools and engagement platforms that are able to go beyond the mere representation of the initiatives of sustainability, through a set of ad hoc targets and key performance indicators, to include processes of mediation among the different stakeholders who are involved. This process requires an integrated approach to the planning, management and reporting that must take into consideration how the interests and the contributions of a series of heterogeneous stakeholders are linked and how they affect the long-term value creation process of a company.

In this chapter, we aim to illustrate the role that Integrated Thinking and Reporting plays in offering a possible platform for businesses to mediate among different parties and resources. In particular, Section 2.2 introduces the recent process of integration of financial and sustainability performance within a company's report. Section 2.3 explores in detail the process of Integrated Thinking and Reporting. Then Section 2.4 illustrates the main guiding principles supporting the preparation of an integrated report and the content to be disclosed. Section 2.5 provides some practical examples of the ways in which Integrated Thinking and Reporting have been performed within organizations. In particular, we will focus on the case of UniCredit Group and SASOL – South Africa. In light of the case studies analysed, Section 2.6 illustrates the key benefits and critics of implementing Integrated Thinking and Reporting. Some further reflections and conclusive remarks are provided in Section 2.7.

2.2. Towards the integration of financial and non-financial performance

In today's interconnected global markets, economic volatility has become the norm and the political, social and environmental risks to which organizations are exposed have continuously increased. This perception has worsened in the aftermath of the recent financial crisis and corporate scandals, in which several commentators and analysts have firmly portrayed the global economic system as being broken, and have viewed organizations as being one of the major causes of social, environmental, and economic problems (Flower, 2015; Gray, 2010; Spence, 2007; Thomson, 2015). This has led many experts, as well as public opinion, to criticize accounting and reporting practices as gradually becoming less fit for the purpose and often failing to shed light on strategy execution as well as on the extensive variety of intangible[1] and natural resources used within an organization's processes of value creation (De Villiers *et al.*, 2014; Dumay *et al.*, 2016; Gray, 2006; 2010; Owen, 2013).

For example, Gray and Milne (2002) argue that current 'accounting for sustainability' practices fail to represent the cumulative effects of organizations' activities on the environment and society because these practices are mainly organization-centred, no matter what is the extent to which they are combined with information on social and environmental impact. Further

---

[1] The value of intangible assets has grown to 84% of total market value for S&P 500 organizations since 1975. http://www.oceantomo.com/2015/03/04/2015-intangible-asset-market-value-study/.

studies have emphasized that organizational reporting practices have often been used as legitimating documents to mask episodes of poor sustainability performance, rather than representing actual facts and managerial actions (O'Dwyer, 2002; Gond *et al.*, 2009; Gray, 2002; 2006; 2010; Milne and Gray, 2007; Spence 2007).

According to O'Dwyer (2002), such skepticism about organizational reporting practices is due to the tendency to provide poor quality disclosures, containing minimal information that is inconsistent with other data reported. Any additional data related to social or environmental issues is perceived as a form of "noise" that distracts managers from their primary objective of maximising economic returns (Gray, 2002, p. 370; see also Gray, 2006). Therefore, accounting and reporting are considered to be poor tools for representing the cumulative effects of organizational activities on social and environmental issues and for supporting collective decision-making on such issues (Gray, 2002).

One of the main reasons for this is that the different aspects of corporate reporting are handled by different standard-settlers (e.g. financial and sustainability reporting), and there has been no overall coordination of how reports should be presented. Further, considering the increasing necessity to understand the role of organizations towards sustainable development, national institutions and regulators have developed guidelines, principles and standards to enhance organizations' accounting and reporting in this regard (for instance, the UN Global Compact, Global Reporting Initiative or Integrated Reporting, etc.).

Although many institutions have attempted to provide guidelines and standards for regulating sustainability reporting, there is still evidence of a mismatch between what an organization says and what they actually do to be sustainable (Higgins *et al.*, 2014). To surpass this mismatch of information, in April 2014, the European Parliament passed a legislative resolution 2014/95/EU regarding the disclosure of non-financial information for large public-interest organizations, (such as listed companies, banks, insurance and other organizations designated by Member States), to increase their transparency in communicating their environmental and social performance and, consequently, to contribute effectively to the long-term economic growth and the employment of a country.

Building on some of the pre-existing developments , at an individual country level in Europe, (see for instance, the UK introduced legislation in 2006 and updated it in 2013; Sweden adopted legislation in 2007; Spain in 2011; Denmark amended its legislation the same year and France in 2012), the European Union Directive 2014/95/EU requires companies with more than 500 employees, 20 million euro of assets and 40 million euro in revenues, to disclose in their management report relevant and useful information about their policies, main risks and outcomes relating to environmental matters; social and employee aspects; respect for human rights; anticorruption and bribery issues; and gender diversity in their board of directors. The aim of this regulation is to provide investors and other stakeholders with a more complete picture of an organization's financial and non-financial, as well as social, environmental and economic performance (European Commission, 2014). The directive also aims to enhance consistency and comparability of nonfinancial information disclosed by organizations within the European Union, while respecting the necessities of organizations to use the most suitable international or national guidelines and approaches for sustainability reporting and corporate social responsibility (Eccles and Spiesshofer, 2015). In this regard, organizations retain significant flexibility for disclosing relevant information in the way that they consider most useful.

Within this context, and in the attempt to offer an account of the ongoing search for competitiveness and sustainable growth featured in contemporary organizations, annual reports are now expected to convey insightful information beyond the traditional key financial data. By identifying and setting ad hoc targets towards sustainable development, management accounting and reporting practices lead the search for sustainable development by stimulating managers, and generally speaking, finance experts, to question the ways in which an organization's value may be converted into added value for a multitude of stakeholders (Busco and Quattrone, 2015).

Positioned at the centre of this debate, *Integrated Reporting* (IR), as an innovative management practice that integrates financial and sustainability performance in a single report, has been portrayed by an emerging body of professional and academic literature as being in a transition of making a leap from a promising concept to a powerful practice (Busco *et al.* 2013a; 2013b; Eccles and Krzus, 2014; 2010). Developed and promoted by the International Integrated Reporting Council (IIRC), IR is presented by its proponents as a process founded on *Integrated Thinking*, which results in a periodic and concise communication about how an organization's strategy, governance, performance and prospects lead to the creation of sustainable value in the short, medium and long term (Adams, 2015; Churet and Eccles, 2015; Adams and Simnett, 2011; Eccles and Krzus, 2014; 2010). Integrated Thinking is a term that refers to the conditions and processes that are conducive to an inclusive process of decision making, management and reporting, based on the connectivity and interdependencies between a range of factors that affect an organization's ability to create value over time (Busco *et al.*, 2017). In the following sections we will go through the main characteristics of integrated reporting and integrated thinking, illustrating the main content elements and guiding principles at the base of the preparation of an integrated report.

2.3. Integrated Reporting and Integrated Thinking

Originally labelled as "One Reporting" by Eccles and Kruzs (2010), the stated goal of *integrated reporting* is to provide information on financial and non-financial performance and their influence on organizations' value creation process in a single document (Owen, 2013). Integrated reporting was initially coined by the International Integrated Reporting Council (IIRC) in 2010 with the aim "to align capital allocation and corporate behaviour to wider goals of financial stability and sustainable development through the cycle of integrated reporting and thinking" [2]. The IIRC was created by professional bodies and business-oriented networks to engage organizations in integrating financial and non-financial information, as well as economic, social and environmental reporting issues (Brown and Dillard, 2014).

In order to spread the purpose and mission of integrated reporting on a larger scale, in September 2011, the IIRC released a Discussion Paper (DP) entitled, "Towards Integrated Reporting – Communicating Value in the 21st Century", to collect suggestions and responses from producers and users of reports to be used as a basis for the development of the International Integrated Reporting Framework. Feedback was collected from a number of businesses and investors who had the opportunity to test the applicability of Integrated Reporting. Following an analysis of the responses to the 2011 Discussion Paper, the IIRC released the first draft of the Integrated Reporting Framework on 11 July 2012. After considering comments from stakeholders on the draft, the IR framework was issued in December 2013.

The framework provides the fundamental concepts, guiding principles, and content elements that govern the overall content of an integrated report. It does not focus on rules for measurement, disclosure of individual matters, or the identification of specific key performance indicators. Instead, the IR framework is principles-based rather than standards-based and is driven by integrated thinking. The idea is to recognize the wide variation in the individual circumstances of different organizations, and, at the same time, enable a sufficient degree of comparability across organizations (Busco *et al.*, 2013a).

---

[2] http://integratedreporting.org/the-iirc-2/.

According to the framework, an integrated report should provide concise information about how an organization's strategy, governance, performance and prospects, in the context of its external environment, lead to the creation of value over the short, medium, and long term (IIRC, 2013, p. 33). An integrated report aims at describing the most material issues that affect an organization and at enhancing accountability and stewardship, with respect to a base of six kinds of capital, or "capitals" (i.e. financial, manufactured, intellectual, human, social and relationship, and natural) (IIRC, 2013, p. 2). It provides information that fulfils the requests of a broader range of stakeholders (e.g. employees, customers, suppliers, partners, local communities, regulators, and policy makers), which are also interested in the organization's ability to create value over time (IIRC, 2013, p. 2).

In this regard, Busco *et al.* (2013a) highlight that an integrated report is not intended to be a set of multiple, isolated pieces of performance information. Instead, it aims at embracing and connecting material information on financial and non-financial performance in order to show how value creation depends on multiple sources of capital. However, as mentioned by Churret and Eccles (2015), an integrated report represents only the crest of an inner process of the collection, connection and communication of performance among different organizations' units and stakeholders. Integrated reporting is the visible part of what is happening below the surface, which the IIRC framework defines as integrated thinking.

The framework defines Integrated Thinking as a fundamental part of the process of integrated reporting. It involves recognizing and managing all the "capitals" that an organization owns and influences, considering the relationships between its various operating and functional units (IIRC, 2013, p. 2). According to the international integrated reporting framework, integrated thinking is "the active consideration by an organisation of the relationships between its various operating and functional units and the capitals that the organisation uses or affects" (p. 2). By practicing integrated thinking, organizations are required to not only achieve stable financial results, but also allocate the right resources, such as, ensuring suitable training for human capital; appropriate manufactured capital as well as ownership or access to the necessary intellectual capital; and explaining the correlations among them (SAICA, 2015). Integrated thinking requires organizations to broaden the range of factors to be taken into account and the actors to be involved in business decision making. This has an effect on the business model and on the strategy of organizations, enabling them to adapt to changes in the external environment and safeguard their longer-term viability.

In particular, integrated thinking is meant to determine: 1) the capitals that the organization uses or affects and the critical interdependencies, including trade-offs, between them; 2) the capacity of the organization to respond to key stakeholders' legitimate needs and interests; 3) how the organization tailors its business model and strategy to respond to its external environment and the risks and opportunities it faces; 4) the organization's activities, performance (financial and other) and outcomes in terms of the capitals – past, present and future (see for instance SAICA, 2015, p. 9).

The more integrated thinking is embedded into an organization's activities, the more naturally will the connectivity of information flow into the reporting and decision-making process. It also leads to better integration of the information systems that support internal and external reporting and communication, including the preparation of the annual integrated report. To improve the comparability of the way in which an integrated report should be structured, the framework provides a set of Fundamental Concepts, Guiding Principles, and Content Elements that represent the structural baseline of any integrated report, which are explained in the following section.

2.3.1. Fundamental concepts

According to the International IR framework, an organization's value creation process is influenced by the external environment; created through relationships with other stakeholders; and is dependent on the availability of various resources (IIRC, 2013, p. 10). Consequently, an integrated report seeks to provide insights about the external environment that affects an organization, the resources and relationships used and affected by the organization (e.g. capitals), as well as the way in which the organization interacts with the external environment and the capitals to create value over the time (IIRC, 2013, p. 10). The fundamental concepts on which the integrated reporting process is built are (1) the capitals that an organization uses and affects, and (2) the value creation process.

The Business Model is the core of the value creation process and is represented by the framework as a system of inputs that are transformed into outputs and outcomes through organizations' business activities (IIRC, 2013, p. 13). The exhibit below (see Exhibit 2.1) shows the so called "octopus", which illustrates inputs as all the resources, relationships and other capitals an organization depends upon or which provide a source of differentiation. These resources are all intertwined and transformed by the different business activities through which an organization creates value for itself and its stakeholders (including society). The framework illustrates outputs as the organization's key products and services as well as any by-products, waste or emissions that affect the external perception of the company, and through which key performances are achieved (Outcomes). The value creation process is cyclical and influences a heterogeneous stock of resources (i.e. capitals) (see Exhibit 2.1).

According to the IR framework, six kinds of capital are generally involved in the value creation process of any organization and can be classified as follows: financial, manufactured, intellectual, human, social and relationship, and natural capital.

The framework refers to *financial capital* as the monetary funds that are used at the disposal of an organization for the production of goods or the provision of services. The *financial capital* includes all funds that are obtained through financing, such as debt, equity or grants, or generated through operations or investments.

Manufactured capital refers to the physical objects or assets (such as equipment, buildings, infrastructure) that are available to an organization for the production of goods or the provision of services.

Intellectual capital comprises all organizational, knowledge-based intangibles, including intellectual property (e.g. patents, copyrights, software, rights and licenses) and "organizational capital" (e.g. tacit knowledge, systems, procedures and protocols).

Human capital relates to the competencies, skills, experiences and capabilities that people hold within organizations and that may improve their innovation process.

Social and relationship capital relates to the relationships that organizations build with local and international institutions; social community groups of stakeholders and other networks, and the ability to share information to enhance individual and collective wellbeing.

Natural capital comprises all renewable and non-renewable environmental resources that are used in the production process of an organization and that support its current or future prosperity.

As mentioned in the framework, however, these capitals are not necessarily fixed, rather they should be tailored according to the organization's value creation process, and they ensure that an organization does not overlook a capital that it uses or affects (IIRC, 2013, p. 12).

The way in which an integrated report should be developed is described in the following sections by exploring the guiding principles and content elements that should be debated throughout the process involved in the preparation of an integrated report.

Exhibit 2.1. The International IR Framework Value Creation Process.

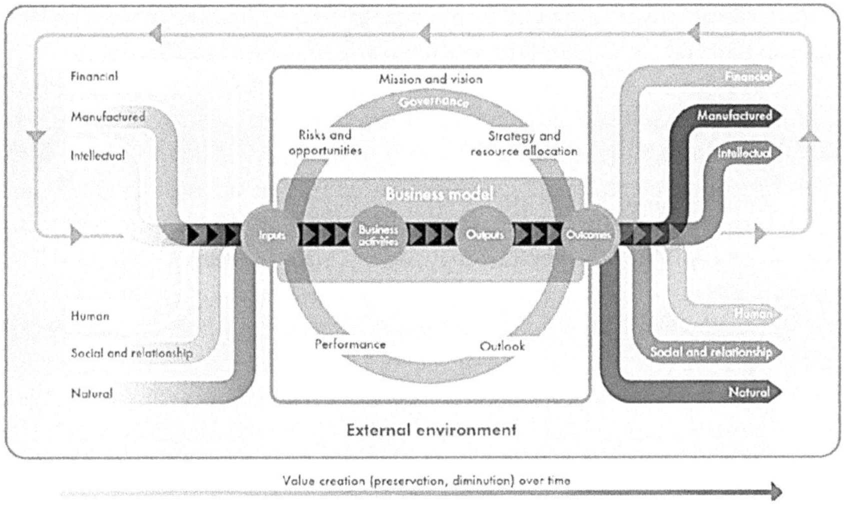

Source: IIRC, 2013, p. 13.

2.3.2. Guiding principles

Because Integrated Reporting aims to offer an appropriate balance between flexibility and prescription, the Framework proposed by the IIRC is principles-based rather than being founded on a more rigid, standards-based approach. The idea is to recognize the variety and different circumstances in which organizations act, independently of their industry and, at the same time, provide guidance on the production of a worldwide accepted integrated report that inevitably requires a sufficient degree of comparability across organizations to meet relevant information needs. For this reason, the IR Framework does not provide standards for the disclosure of certain matters or even the identification of specific key performance indicators. Rather, it provides a set of six guiding principles to stimulate organizations' active consideration of the relationships between their various operating and functional units and the kinds of capital that they use and affect.

The six guiding principles on which any published integrated report should be based on are: *strategic focus and future orientation*; *connectivity of information*; *stakeholder responsiveness*; *materiality and conciseness*; *reliability and completeness*; *consistency and comparability* (IIRC, 2013, p. 16).

The first principle, *strategic focus and future orientation*, refers to the selection and presentation of a series of aspects that are related to an organization's strategy. It may include opportunities, risks and dependencies flowing from the organization's market position and business model; past and future performances; the balance among short-, medium- and long-term interests and perspectives, as well as the evaluation of past performance that may influence future strategies (IIRC, 2013, p. 16).

The principle of *Connectivity of information* seeks to provide a holistic picture of the combination, interrelatedness and dependencies between the factors that affect the organization's ability to create value over time. It involves recognizing and managing all the capitals that the business owns and influences, considering the relationships between its various operating and functional units and the capitals that the organization uses or affects (IIRC, 2013).

The principle of *Stakeholder responsiveness* reflects the relevance of creating valuable relationships among the organizations' key stakeholders. According to the framework, building reliable relationships with stakeholders may assist organizations in better understanding how stakeholders perceive value; identify future trends that may not yet have come to general attention, but which are rising in significance; identify material opportunities and risks; develop and evaluate strategy; manage risks; and implement strategic responses to material matters. Furthermore, the framework suggests that engaging with stakeholders on a regular basis should enhance an organization's accountability and transparency.

The fourth principle is *Materiality*. The framework defines a matter as being material if it has "or may have, an effect on the organization's ability to create value. This is determined by considering effects on the organization's strategy, governance, performance or prospects" (IIRC, 2013, p. 18). The determination of materiality involves: identifying relevant matters based on their ability to affect value creation; evaluating the importance of such matters in terms of their known or potential effect on value creation; prioritizing the matters based on their relative importance and determining the information to disclose about material matters.[3] The framework explains that the materiality determination process is applicable to both positive and negative matters (e.g., opportunities and risks, and favorable and un-favorable results or prospects for the future), as well as to financial and non-financial information that has direct implications for the organization itself or that may affect the capitals owned by or available to others.

Another principle is *Conciseness*. This principle requires that an integrated report provides enough information on the organization's strategy, governance, performance and prospects without being burdened with less

[3] For more detailed information on the Materiality Determination Process, please refer to the International IR Framework, pp. 18-20.

relevant information. However, this is not synonymous with incomplete information.

The *reliability and completeness of information* highlights that an integrated report should provide the right balance between positive and negative material matters. The framework refers to reliability as the characteristic of a report that can be enhanced by mechanisms such as strong internal control and reporting systems, appropriate stakeholder engagement and independent, internal audit or similar functions, as well as external assurance (IIRC, 2013, p. 21). As for completeness, the framework suggests that a complete integrated report should include all material information, both positive and negative, that could affect the organization's ability to create value.

Then, *consistency and comparability* conclude the section dedicated to the guiding principles that underpin the integrated reporting process. According to the IR Framework, the information presented in an integrated report should be consistent over time and enable comparison with other organizations to the extent that the aspects reported are material to the organization's own ability to create value over time (IIRC, 2013, p. 23).

2.3.3. Content elements

An integrated report consists of eight elements that are relevant for communicating an organization's unique value-creation story (Busco *et al.* 2013a). According to the framework, the content elements of an integrated report are as follows: *the organizational overview and external environment*; *governance*; *business model*; *risks and opportunities*; *strategy and resource allocation*; *performance*; *future outlook*; and the *basis of preparation and presentation*. However, the framework indicates that content elements should not be represented separately but linked together to better illustrate the cause-effect relationship between the multiple financial and non-financial resources employed in the company's value creation process. The eight elements are not intended to serve as a standard structure for an integrated report, but should be tailored to an organization's individual circumstances, enhancing communication among different stakeholders. As highlighted by Busco *et al.* (2013a), such flexibility has a key role in stimulating a process of integrated thinking within organizations, requiring managers from different functions (such as sustainability, finance and control, risk management, communication, logistics, external relations, etc.) to question and discuss the most material issues that affect the short-, medium- and long-term impacts of the business. For this reason, the IR framework's *Content Elements* are presented in the form of questions, rather than being a checklist of specific disclosures (IIRC, 2013, p. 24).

The first of the content elements presented in the IR framework is the *Organizational Overview and External Environment.* It asks organizations to describe the business and the circumstances in which it operates, providing information about the organization's mission and vision; its culture, ethics and values; ownership and operating structure; principal markets; products and activities; as well as the competitive landscape and market positioning (IIRC, 2011, pp. 24-25).

In terms of *Governance,* an integrated report should provide insights into how an organization's governance structure supports its ability to create value in the short, medium, and long term. This should include information about the leadership structure; the specific processes used to make strategic decisions; the strategic direction and approach to risk management; and additionally, how culture, ethics, and values affect capitals (IIRC, 2013, p. 25).

The *Business Model* represents the core element of an integrated report. An integrated report aims to describe the most material inputs of its value creation process and how they relate to the capitals from which they were derived. This includes key business activities, such as how the organization differentiates itself in the market, approaches innovation and adapts to change. Finally, outcomes describe how internal and external stakeholders perceive the organization's actions.

The content element *Opportunities and Risks* should define the key financial and non-financial risks and opportunities that are specific to an organization, identifying the specific sources of risk; assessing the likelihood that the risk or opportunity will come to fruition and the magnitude of its effect; determining the most adequate mitigating actions to reduce their impact on the organization's strategies (IIRC, 2013, p. 26).

The fifth element described in the IR Framework is *Strategy and Resource Allocation.* It seeks to describe where an organization wants to go and how it intends to get there. In other words, an integrated report is intended to inform users of the organization's short-, medium- and long-term strategic objectives; the resource allocation plans it has in place to implement its strategy; as well as the targeted outcomes for the short-, medium- and long-term (IIRC, 2013, p. 26).

Outcomes and targets are described through the content element *Performance.* According to the framework, an integrated report should contain quantitative and qualitative information about performance on matters such as risks and opportunities, the organization's effects on the capitals, the state of key stakeholder relationships and the links between past, present and anticipated future targets.

According to the framework, organizations' strategies, performance and risks should be described through a prospective *Outlook*. In this regard, an integrated report should provide information on the organization's expectations about the external environment in the short-, medium- and long-term, explaining how the organization is equipped to respond to the critical challenges and uncertainties that are likely to arise.

Finally, the last content element, the *Basis of Preparation and Presentation,* requires organizations to explain the way in which they have defined their choice of which elements to include in the report and the frameworks and methods used to quantify or evaluate material matters (IIRC, 2013, p. 29).

As we have already mentioned in this chapter, all the content disclosed in an integrated report should be interconnected, inviting different organizational functions and stakeholders to question the most relevant issues to illustrate and communicate. At the base of this questioning and debating process, Integrated Thinking and Reporting require that organizations re-think their traditional accounting and reporting practices towards the integration and understanding of the financial and non-financial sources of capital that affect their capacity to create sustainable value in the short-, medium- and long-term.

The following section illustrates the case of two multinational companies, UniCredit Group and SASOL South Africa, explaining how Integrated Thinking and Reporting have been approached and developed in two different sectors, located in two different countries (Italy and South Africa).

Although the analysis of the structure and content of the integrated reports of UniCredit and SASOL would be relevant for understanding their commitment to the guidelines suggested by the IIRC framework, in this chapter we focus on the connectivity principles and the key practices that better illustrate how integrated thinking is performed in practice in the two organizations under analysis.

2.4. Integrated Thinking in practice: cases and best practices

2.4.1. UniCredit Group

The UniCredit Group is one of the first European banks to pioneer Integrated Thinking and Reporting. It employs over 140,000 employees and is a fully plugged-in Corporate and Investment Bank, delivering its services to an extensive network of 25 million clients. As a provider of banking services in 14 countries, UniCredit is closely tied to the lifeblood of many national economies.

In line with the most recent international developments in corporate reporting, since 2014 the Group has continued to report on sustainability through its Integrated Report, which aims to describe the Group's financial and sustainability performance, business model, corporate governance, risk management, compliance, competitive environment, strategy and capitals (UniCredit, 2016). The Report was produced in accordance with the disposition of the Group CEO and is managed by the Group Sustainability function, in collaboration with the Strategy, Business Development and management accounting functions.

In accordance with the guidelines set out by "International <IR> Framework", the "G4 Sustainability Reporting Guidelines" and the main "Financial Services Sector Disclosures", the 2016 Integrated Report of UniCredit provides information about the past, present and future strategic priorities of the company and its sustainability performance in the long run. In particular the UniCredit Integrated Report of 2016 represents its integrated thinking by showing the main interdependent relationship between the organization's strategies, business activities and capitals, required to better illustrate the changing needs and expectations of the stakeholders towards a shared value creation approach.

The report clearly maintains that the main objective of UniCredit as a Pan European Bank is to be a positive example of how a private business can fully embrace its duty to generate shared values that are linked with social and economic progress (UniCredit, 2016, p. 69).

Through the business model, UniCredit's 2016 Integrated Report illustrates the main company's strategic objectives (e.g. five fundamentals), the main banking activities (e.g. commercial banking and corporate & investment banking), the different sources of capital on which the bank depends (e.g. five capitals such as the financial, human, intellectual, social and relationship, natural capitals), and the key performance achieved during the year in terms of the values and impacts of sustainable development (Economic, Social and Environmental Values).

Through its business model the bank aims to illustrate how multiple financial and non-financial resources and relationships are correlated and converted into outputs and outcomes that are relevant for achieving the organization's strategies and targets in the short-, medium- and long-term (see Exhibit 2.2).

To better understand the main issues that affect the company's value creation process, UniCredit regularly invests in developing engagement initiatives that embrace a variety of stakeholders. As part of these continuous dialogues with the main stakeholders, through integrated reporting UniCredit has been able to identify and assess the most relevant topics that forge its business strategy and viability. Through this process, UniCredit develops a materiality analysis according to the guidelines provided by the Global Reporting Initiative. The resulting matrix that emerges from the analysis compares the main organization's stakeholder needs and expectations in accordance with the company's main targets and strategic objectives.

Exhibit 2.2. UniCredit Business Model.

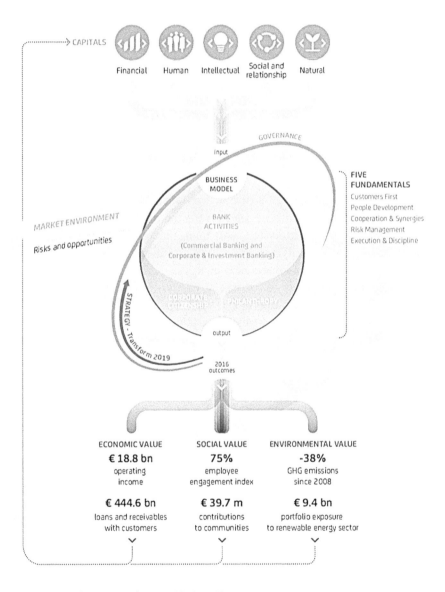

Source: UniCredit Integrated Report 2016, p. 10.

In 2016, the traditional materiality matrix was reviewed to better illustrate the correlations between the company's most relevant issues and the main stakeholder needs. In particular, the materiality analysis was developed in four main phases, through which the company (UniCredit, 2016, p. 29):

• maps and prioritizes the main stakeholders by relevance, according to their economic dependence, ability to influence and the relative urgency with which the company must encounter their expectations;
• identifies the most relevant issues using benchmarks; sustainability rating agencies; social media; listening and engaging tools, scenario analyses, etc.;
• prioritizes the identified issues according to the feedback gathered through the stakeholder engagement initiatives;
• assesses internal consensus on the issues that are most important for the organization's stakeholders by engaging with the group functions that manage their requests.

The issues considered to be relevant for the organization's stakeholders and the macro trends associated with them (such as big data, population growth, aging societies, hyperconnectivity, global warming) were also integrated into the company's materiality analysis.

Concerning the trends of increasing customer connectivity (hyperconnectivity) and the digitalization of the bank, the 2016 UniCredit integrated report illustrates the investment made and the results achieved in Italy. The Italian case study shows how two of the main activities of the bank, such as retail and private banking, have been improved, illustrating the capitals employed in this process, connecting a wide range of factors, and explaining how each of these interconnections contributed to the achievement of good results at the end of the year (e.g. by increasing of number of customers and increasing the number of online banking users).

To improve the digitalization process of the bank in Italy, the group made significant investments in enhancing the skills of its human resources and intellectual capital. A project entitled *Open in Action* was launched to facilitate the transformation of the core activities of the bank in the retail and private banking segments. The project utilizes an integrated, three-partite approach, that involves: 1) a dedicated team of professionals to identify unresolved issues; 2) an online platform created to facilitate communications across a broad network and reinforce colleague engagement; 3) and a service model monitoring the program's progress. These approaches are aligned with the company's strategic objectives and translated into quantitative performance that reflects the impact of financial and social and relational capitals (e.g. percentage of new customers; percentage of new online banking users)

One of UniCredit's most relevant approaches to the assessment of the different capitals that affect and are affected by the main bank's traditional initiatives relates to a methodological approach entitled, the "Evolution economy". This methodology explores the shared value generated by its core business activities, citizenship initiatives and philanthropic projects. Furthermore, this methodology considers 97 indicators, chosen from the most relevant international statistical institutions, such as BES and the Italian National Institute of Statistics, the OECD Better Life Index, and the WEF Global Competitiveness Index.

Through these indicators UniCredit assesses the most problematic issues of the seven countries in which it operates in Europe, analyzing the trends of the last ten years, their deviation from EU averages and top performers. This methodological approach provides a picture of the UniCredit countries' most relevant priorities for financial and social well-being, security, education, health, economy, environment and productivity, to name only a few. By adopting this approach, UniCredit targets the continuous interactions between the company and its operating environment in order to understand the conditions in which people live as well as how local companies operate and, thus, formulate a clear plan for development in the long run.

Through this methodology, UniCredit aims to increase internal and external awareness of the shared value that is generated by its business activities; increase consciousness regarding the coherence between vision and initiatives; align internal communication and enhance engagement and participation, as well as support group positioning and reputation through external communication by enriching the narration of its existing activities (see Exhibit 2.3).

Exhibit 2.3. Analysis of Country priorities in UniCredit.

Country Priorities

High | Medium | Low

Macro Dimension	Indicator	Italy	Germany	Austria	CEE^
Social Wellbeing	Employment rate of people 20-64 years	Medium	Low	Low	Low
	Social decay (or incivilities) rate	High	Medium	Medium	Medium
	Work satisfaction	Medium	Low	Low	Low
	Citizens who benefit from infancy services	High	Low	Medium	High
Economic Wellbeing	People suffering poor housing conditions	High	Medium	High	Medium
	Severely materially deprived people	High	Low	Low	Medium
	Index of subjective evaluation of economic distress	High	Medium	Medium	High
Education and Efficient use of talent	Country capacity to attract talent	Medium	Low	Medium	Medium
	Percentage of young people not in education, employment, or training (NEET)	High	Low	Low	High
	Percentage of people participating in formal or non-formal education	Medium	Medium	Low	Medium
Health	Healthy life expectancy at birth	Low	Medium	Medium	Medium
	Waiting lists	High	Low	Low	Medium
	Life expectancy without activity limitations at 65 years of age	High	High	Medium	Medium
Environment & Landscape	Energy from renewable sources	Low	Medium	Low	Low
	Public expenditure for recreation, culture and religion	High	High	Medium	Low
	Emissions of CO_2 per inhabitant	Low	Medium	Low	Low
Infrastructure & Quality of services	Quality of overall infrastructure	Medium	Medium	Medium	Low
	Quality of roads	Low	Medium	Low	Low
	Internet bandwidth	Medium	Medium	High	Medium
Financial Market	Availability of financial services	Medium	Medium	Medium	Low
	Ease of access to loans	High	Low	Medium	Medium
	Venture capital availability	High	Low	High	Low
Business Sophistication	Local supplier quality	Low	Low	Medium	Low
	Extent of marketing	Medium	Low	Low	Low
	Nature of competitive advantage	Low	Low	Low	Medium
Innovation	Innovation rate of the national productive system	Medium	Medium	Low	Medium
	Research intensity	Medium	Low	Low	Medium
	Patent propensity	High	Medium	Low	Medium

Source: UniCredit Integrated Report 2016, p. 70.

Furthermore, a snapshot of the key sectors in Italy that are primarily affected by UniCredit's initiatives is illustrated in the report, describing the country's priorities that have been impacted by these initiatives. In particular, the integrated report focuses on sectors such as tourism, agriculture and infrastructure, which represent the backbone of Italian competitiveness, social welfare and culture. Exhibit 2.4 shows UniCredit's projects, KPISs and main impacts for the infrastructure sector in Italy.

Exhibit 2.4. UniCredit initiatives, KPIs and Impacts in the infrastructure sector.

Projects	Expected effects on territories[a]	Priorities impacted
> Health		
• 14 hospitals	• 15 provinces served • around 13 million potential beneficiaries[c] • more than 9,000 beds provided	• waiting lists • quality of overall infrastructure
> Motorways		
• 4 motorways	• 520 km of motorways constructed and redeveloped (around 9 percent of total motorways in Italy)[b] • average traffic flow of 380 million vehicles per km every month (5 percent of total Italian traffic flow per month)[b]	• quality of road infrastructure • traffic accidents
• 1 project to redevelop 103 tunnels for the network of state highways in Lombardy (Strade Statali, SS)	• 138 km of SS tunnels, representing 96 percent all SS tunnels in Lombardy	
> Logistics		
• 1 new parking lot in Rho Fiera (the largest Trade Fair Center in Italy per m², the seventh-most revenues in the EU; it averages 5 million visitors per year)	• 10,000 new parking spaces in Rho Fiera	• quality of overall infrastructure • local supplier quality and quantity
• 2 new office buildings, for Bologna municipality and Emilia Romagna region	• over 20 municipal offices centralized • 1,000 employees transferred to new Bologna Municipality building • 3 regional departments consolidated • 600 employees transferred to new building for Emilia Romagna region	
• redevelopment of the Mercato Trionfale in Rome	• over 265 commercial spaces • 390 refurbished parking spaces	
> Water		
• redevelopment of 3 water service networks	• 11 provinces served • around 200 municipalities served • roughly 2 million beneficiaries[c]	• quality of overall infrastructure
> Metro		
• 2 metro lines (M5 & M4) in Milan	• over 6 km and 10 stations added to M5 line • 236 percent increase in M5 line passengers between April and October 2015 • 2 percent CO_2 emission reduction (forecast) • reduction of roughly 30 million cars on city roads (forecast)	• emission of CO_2 per inhabitant • quality of overall infrastructure

Source: UniCredit Integrated Report 2016, p. 75.

2.4.2. SASOL South Africa

With over 50 years' experience in the production and marketing of a range of chemicals, SASOL is one of the world's largest producers of synthetic fuels, gas-to-liquids (GTL), coal-to-liquids (CTL) and related technologies, with more than 30,000 people working in 33 countries.

With the King III principles included in the JSE listing requirements on an "apply or explain" basis, the most listed companies in South Africa have been required to prepare an integrated report since 2011. As a South African company listed on the Johannesburg Stock Exchange (JSE), one of the drivers of Integrated Thinking and Reporting within SASOL has been compliance to the King Code of Corporate Governance.

In its 2016 integrated report, SASOL connects key inputs to business model activities (namely, natural and intellectual capital), outputs and outcomes, explaining its value creation process and governance structure. To respond appropriately to the changing business and risk landscape, SASOL represents its business model as an integration of the key elements of the strategy, the operating model, the technology advantage, the most material issues and performance. In particular, the Business Model is represented over two pages spreads.

The first page illustrates the six capitals as inputs, the activities taken to manage these resources, their effects on strategies and the nature of some of the trade-offs between the capitals in accordance with the principles issued by the IIRC International <IR> Framework. At the end of the process, some additional information is provided regarding the financial and sustainability performance achieved during the year and the value distributed to a variety of stakeholders such as employees, governments, shareholders, and the community as a whole. The second spread illustrates the outcomes achieved and the value distributed to the different organizational stakeholders in relation to each of the six capitals involved in the company's value creation process. The performances achieved per capital are commented in boxes, illustrating the actions taken to enhance outcomes for stakeholders and comparing them to the previous year. An additional column provides deeper insights into the model by discussing the 'trade-offs' associated with the capitals influenced by SASOL. These concepts are introduced and illustrated in a diagram and discussed further in the report's narrative. (see Exhibit 2.5)

Exhibit 2.5. SASOL Business Model.

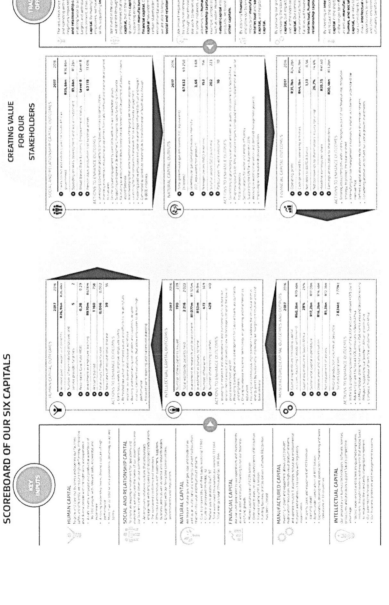

Source: SASOL S.A. Integrated Report 2017, pp. 12-13.

To strengthen the integrated thinking process and connectivity of information within the company's integrated report, SASOL provides a performance scorecard through which the organization illustrates the progress against seven Key Performance Indicators (KPIs) that are linked to the delivery of financial and sustainability strategies in the long run, (e.g. ROIC, Quality Based Earnings Growth, Net Debt to EBITDA, Gearing, Safety, Greenhouse gas emissions, Broad Base Black Economic Empowerment), and establish the basement for the organization's manager remuneration policy (see Exhibit 2.6).

Exhibit 2.6. SASOL Performance Scorecard.

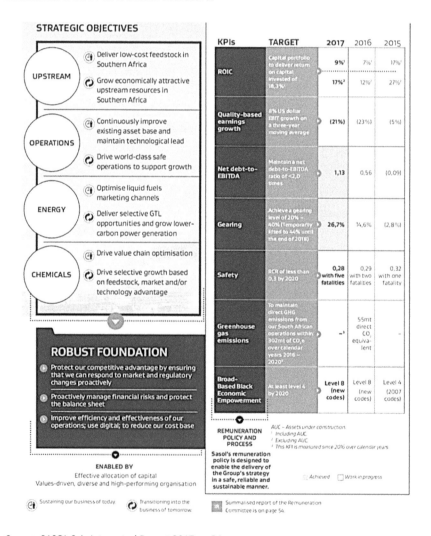

In their 2017 integrated report, SASOL clearly illustrates the main stakeholders' engagement initiatives, explaining for each of them the relevance to the organization's perimeter. Stakeholders are identified according to the environment they are related to and the issues considered to be material for them. Further, SASOL's Integrated report 2017 illustrates how the company's approach to integrated thinking has contributed to the materiality assessment process by focusing on the five most relevant material matters (e.g. Macro-economic Environment; Delivering Value-based Growth; Human Capital Management; Environmental Sustainability; Commitment to our communities) that are considered as affecting the ability of the company to create value in the short, medium or long term.

For each of the five matters considered to be relevant for the organization's strategies, the integrated report 2017 discusses the main initiatives undertaken to achieve and improve them. Furthermore, for the first time the report illustrates the trade-off relations among the different capitals involved in this initiative. Throughout the evaluation process of the material matters that affect the company's ability to create sustainable value in the long run, the board played a relevant role and has been considered determinant in fostering integrated thinking, interrogating the company's strategy and potentially driving innovation.

2.5. Benefits and critics of Integrated Thinking and Reporting

The framework considers Integrated Thinking and Reporting as two sides of the same coin and are both required to increase the connectivity of the information and communication of the performance that affects an organization's ability to create sustainable value.

Integrated reporting and integrated thinking require companies to broaden their focus from traditional reporting models, by using a more connected approach and understanding of how the financial and non-financial sources of capital that a business uses can be strategic to the achievement of long-term sustainable value creation. This provides a foundation from which to discuss the performance, prospects and governance of the business in a way that focuses on its most important aspects (Busco *et al.*, 2013b). Moreover, it supports decision making at management and board levels, more focused reporting and enhanced communication with stakeholders.

As highlighted in the case studies described, the process of Integrated Thinking and Reporting requires a continuous connection and interaction among different perspectives and a more cohesive management information system to analyse and collect, and possibly improve, the accountability and communication of multiple performances. Nowadays, managers have access to a higher number and variety of information than before. This greater volume of information, often labelled as Big Data, has the potential to improve or deflect the future directions and performance of an organization. Thus, by adopting integrated thinking and reporting, organizations are expected to positively improve the reliability of the information provided, but also the decision-making process within organizations (IIRC, 2013).

However, to full exploit the potential of this variety of information, organizations are required to invest significantly in sophisticated analytics tools that are able to turn raw and often unstructured information into strategic insight, driving competitive advantage and managing risk (SAICA, 2015). The implementation of these innovative tools may help to ensure that information is readily available to people across the organization, fostering the sharing of information and promoting interactions among different units within the organization.

These continuous interactions among different actors within the organization may improve data analysis and its prioritization in order to carefully recognize how internal and external resources are employed and determine whether they are relevant to an organization's value creation process or not. Further, the identification of the best way to allocate resources may enhance the accountability of the information provided by focusing on more efficient capital flows and better quality of dialogue with stakeholders and driving new investments and productivity.

Although IR is meant to mobilize a large amount of corporate information, facilitating engagement and activism from the organization's internal and external stakeholders, some critics have recently emerged (Eccles and Serafeim, 2013; Owen, 2013; Busco *et al.* 2013a). IR adopters and users still face constraints on the determination of the information that an integrated report should contain, as well as its materiality for the overall organization's value creation. For instance, Flower (2015) sustains that the IIRC concept of value creation is too vague and largely oriented toward an organization's investors' requests, rather than the broader communities of stakeholders. According to Higgins *et al.* (2014), the narratives on sustainability produced by integrated reports are often deployed in relation to organizational perspectives and shareholder-driven purposes. Moreover, the persuasive (i.e. rhetorical) "story-telling" of integrated reporting on sustainability make it a fascinating practice that is increasingly adopted by private and public organizations to meet strategic drivers and institutional expectations, as opposed to social and environmental issues (Higgins *et al.* 2014).

Also, Zappettini and Unerman (2016) maintain that IR refers to sustainability as a discourse often constructed around internal organization speculations, more than external and holistic discursive orientations. In this regard, IR provides a way of making sustainability impacts measurable in financial terms and aims at maximizing long-run shareholder value by indicating how an organization's mission, objectives, strategies, performance measurement systems and indicators integrate with each other (Brown and Dillard, 2014).

Also, the evaluation of the most relevant aspects that "have, or may have, an effect on the organization's ability to create value", and likewise of the capitals that an organization exploits or affects, may be biased to the extent that they are inputs to the organization's production process (Flower, 2015). For these reasons, Humphrey *et al.* (2016) maintain that such ambiguity about the aims of the IIRC make integrated reporting an appealing idea not so much because of its innovativeness or because of its openness to various stakeholders, but because different parties and interest groups can all construct their integrated report in a way that makes it attractive to them. Furthermore, the lack of standards in IR for nonfinancial information make different companies' performance difficult to compare, and raise questions regarding the reliability, consistency and completeness of the information presented in an integrated report (Brown and Dillard, 2014; Flower, 2015).

Despite these criticisms, there is confidence among practitioners and academics that Integrated Thinking and Reporting may turn out to be an important step towards the integration of long-term sustainable development objectives. Within this context, and in an attempt to offer an account of the ongoing search for competitiveness and sustainable growth featured in contemporary organizations, Integrated Thinking and Reporting are expected to stimulate informed decisions and wise interrogations into how an organization should create sustainable value.

2.6. Summary and conclusions

Whether recent critical academic and professional studies present Integrated Thinking and Reporting as a possible rational choice for facing existing challenges, or a ceremonial response to the increasing pressures of markets and society, or a temporary fad and fashion (Higgins *et al.*, 2014; van Bommel, 2014; Brown and Dillard, 2014), this research project acknowledges that this novel form of reporting has rapidly gained considerable prominence as one of the main management and accounting innovations of the recent decade (Adams, 2015; Churet and Eccles, 2015; Adams and

Simnett, 2011; Eccles and Krzus, 2014). And this trend is due to continue, with several organizations adopting integrated thinking as a basis for fostering internal processes of change. The main challenges concern identifying useful, reliable indicators, reporting them consistently and gaining buy-in from internal and external stakeholders.

This outside-in perspective aids management to develop a more holistic view of their business and its operating context. A growing number of organizations already understand the value of a more direct dialogue with their stakeholders and are taking steps to achieve it. In this way they also gain greater understanding of how external stakeholders perceive the impact the business is having, both in financial and other terms (PwC, 2016).

Within this context, the finance unit takes the centre of the stage, acting as orchestrator of a process of thinking, measuring and reporting that mediates among multiple concerns, facilitates conversations, and fosters a generation of innovative solutions within contexts that are characterized by multiple interests, backgrounds and points of view (Busco *et al.*, 2015).

2.7. References

Adams, C.A., (2015), "The international integrated reporting council: a call to action". *Critical Perspectives on Accounting*, Vol. 27, pp. 23-28.

Brown, J., and Dillard, J., (2014), "Integrated reporting: On the need for broadening out and opening up", Accounting, Auditing & Accountability Journal, Vol. 27 No. 7, pp. 1120-1156.

Busco C., Frigo, M.L., Quattrone, P. and Riccaboni, A., (2013a), *Towards integrated reporting: concepts, elements and principles*, Springer, London, UK.

Busco C., Frigo, M.L., Quattrone, P. and Riccaboni, A., (2013b), "Redefining corporate accountability through integrated reporting: What happens when values and value creation meet?", *Strategic Finance* Vol. 95 No. 2, pp. 33-42.

Busco, C., and Quattrone, P. (2017), "In Search of the "Perfect One": How accounting as a maieutic machine sustains inventions through generative 'intensions'". *Management Accounting Research*, (*in press*)

de Villiers, C., Rinaldi, L., Unerman, J., (2014), "Integrated Reporting: Insights, gaps and an agenda for future research", *Accounting, Auditing & Accountability Journal*, Vol. 27 No. 7, pp. 1042-1067.

Dumay, J., Bernardi, C., Guthrie, J., Demartini, P., (2016), "Integrated reporting: A structured literature review", *Accounting Forum*, Vol. 40, No. 3, pp. 166-185.

Eccles, R.G., and Krzus, M.P., (2010), *One Report: Integrated Reporting for a Sustainable* Strategy, John Wiley & Sons, Hoboken, NJ.

Eccles, R.G., and Krzus, M.P., (2014), *The integrated reporting movement*, John Wiley & Sons.

Eccles, R.G., and Serafeim, G. (2013), "The performance frontier", *Harvard business review*, Vol. 91 No. 5, pp. 50-60.

Eccles, R.G. and Spiesshofer, B., (2015), "Integrated Reporting for a Re-Imagined Capitalism", *Harvard Business Review,* Working Paper 16-032, pp. 1-24.

Flower, J., (2015), "The International Integrated Reporting Council: a story of failure", *Critical Perspectives on Accounting*, Vol. 27, pp. 1-17.

Gond, J.P., Palazzo, G. and Basu, K. (2009), "Reconsidering instrumental corporate social responsibility through the Mafia metaphor" *Business Ethics Quarterly*, Vol. 19 No. 1, pp. 57-85.

Gray, R. (2002), "Of Messiness, Systems and Sustainability: Towards a more Social and Environmental Finance and Accounting", *British Accounting Review*, Vol. 34, pp. 357-386.

Gray, R. (2006), "Social, environmental and sustainability reporting and organisational value creation? Whose value? Whose creation?" *Accounting, Auditing & Accountability Journal*, Vol. 19 No. 6, pp. 793-819.

Gray, R. (2010), "Is accounting for sustainability actually accounting for sustainability…and how would we know? An exploration of narratives of organisations and the planet", *Accounting, Organizations and Society*, Vol. 35 No. 1, pp. 47-62.

Gray, R. and Milne, M. (2002), "Sustainability Reporting: Who's Kidding Whom?" *Chartered Accountants Journal of New Zealand*, Vol. 81 No .6, pp. 66-70.

Higgins, C., Stubbs, W., and Love, T., (2014), "Walking the talk(s): Organisational narratives of integrated reporting", *Accounting, Auditing & Accountability Journal*, Vol. 27 No. 7, pp. 1090-1119.

IIRC (2013), International <IR> framework, http: //integrate-dreporting.org/resources/.

Milne, M., and Gray, R.H. (2007), "Future prospects for corporate sustainability reporting", In J. Unerman, J. Bebbington, and B. O'Dwyer (Eds.), *Sustainability accounting and accountability*, Routledge Taylor and Francis Group, London, Uk, pp. 184-208.

Owen, G. (2013), "Integrated reporting: a review of developments and their implications for the accounting curriculum", *Accounting Education*, Vol. 22 No. 4, pp. 340-356.

Price Waterhouse Cooper – PwC (2015). Make it your business: Engaging with the Sustainable Development Goals, https://www.pwc.com/gx/en/sustainability/SDG/SDG%20Research_FINAL.pdf Accessed 27 January 2018.

Sasol S.A. (2017), Integrated report, pp. 1-46. http://www.sasol.com/extras/IR_2017/ Accessed 27 January 2018.

Serafeim, G., (2015), "Integrated Reporting and Investor Clientele", Journal of Applied Corporate Finance, Vol. 27 No. 2, pp. 34-51.

Simnett, R., and Huggins, A.L., (2015), "Integrated reporting and assurance: where can research add value?", Sustainability Accounting, Management and Policy Journal, Vol. 6 No. 1, pp. 29-53.

Spence, C. (2007), "Social and environmental reporting and hegemonic discourse", *Accounting, Auditing and Accountability Journal*, Vol. 20 No. 6, pp. 855-882.

Thomson, I., (2015), "But Does Sustainability need Capitalism or an Integrated Report a Commentary on 'The International Integrated Reporting Council: A Story of Failure" by Flower, J., *Critical Perspectives on Accounting,* Vol. 27, pp. 18-22.

van Bommel, K., (2014), "Towards a legitimate compromise? an exploration of Integrated Reporting in the Netherlands", Accounting, Auditing & Accountability Journal, Vol. 27 No. 7, pp. 1157-1189.

UniCredit (2016 a), Integrated Report 2016. https://www.unicreditgroup.eu/content/dam/unicreditgroup-eu/documents/en/sustainability/sustainability-reports/2016/2016-Integrated-Report_interactive_13042017.pdf Accessed 27 January 2018.

UniCredit (2016 b), Paper Evolution Economy, https://www.unicreditgroup.eu/content/dam/unicreditgroup-eu/documents/it/sustainability/our-vision-of-a-sustainable-bank/Paper_Evolution_Economy_nov2016.pdf Accessed 27 January 2018.

Chapter 3

SUSTAINABLE DEVELOPMENT GOALS: A NEW ROLE FOR ORGANIZATIONS

by *Maria Federica Izzo*

SUMMARY: 3.1. Introduction. – 3.2. Redefining sustainable growth. – 3.3. The road toward Sustainable Development Goals. – 3.4. The Sustainable Development Goals. – 3.5. A new role for organizations. – 3.6. How companies make SDGs happen: cases and best practices. – 3.6.1. Iberdrola: the alignment between strategy and the SDGs. – 3.6.2. Electrolux: For the Better. – 3.7. The role of management accountants in making SDGs happen. – 3.8. Summary and conclusions. – 3.9. References.

3.1. Introduction

The United Nations Rio+20 summit in Brazil in 2012 committed governments to identify a set of Sustainable Development Goals (SDGs) that would be integrated into the follow-up of the Millennium Development Goals (MDGs) after their 2015 deadline, and which, hopefully, would overcome their shortfalls. Therefore, the SDGs represent a new, coherent way of thinking about how issues as diverse as poverty, education and climate change fit together. They twist economic, social and environmental aspects into 17 goals that aim to achieve a critical set of important social priorities at a global level, which eventually require active worldwide public and private participation, as well as political focus.

The ideas and challenges presented by the SDGs have immediately gained ground in different milieu because of the growing urgency for sustainable development and the widespread debate about the so-called Anthropocene.

Following the work of the Nobel Prize-winning author, Paul Crutzen, the term Anthropocene denotes the current geological era in which "human activity is pushing crucial global ecosystem functions past a dangerous threshold, beyond which the earth might well encounter abrupt, highly non-linear, and potentially devastating outcomes for human wellbeing and life generally" (Sachs, 2012).

The present era is distinguished by the fact that human activity has caused not only one, but many, overlapping crises involving environmental sustainability. Among other effects, the emissions of greenhouse gases and massive environmental pollution have caused and critically impacted the climate change process. Moreover, the never-ending conversion of forests into farms and pastures has provoked the massive loss of biodiversity and the uncontrollable increase in the production rate has been implicated in the depletion of key fossil resources, such as oil, gas, coal and groundwater.

According to the United Nations Secretary-General Ban Ki-moon, in this dire scenario business is a vital partner in achieving the Sustainable Development Goals, since the public sector alone cannot address this challenge.

Sustainability requires the leadership and responsibility of the private sector together with the public sector and civil society.

In this sense, companies can contribute to this common set of goals and targets through their core activities (they hold much of the advanced technologies and management systems that will be crucial for the success of the SDGs) and, at the same time, they are invited to assess their impact, set ambitious goals and communicate their results in a transparent way. SDGs, then, also rely on the important and value-creating role of business organizations in delivering the promise of sustainable and inclusive development.

The business sector's contribution to SDGs can be obtained by both maximizing the positive impacts of their practices and by minimizing the negative impacts on the population and the planet.

SDGs, in fact, can act as both an opportunity and as a challenge. Several business organizations across the globe have started this journey by identifying and executing sustainable strategies as key drivers of their visions and business models. The SDGs offer an opportunity for business-led solutions and technologies to be developed, and they offer an overarching framework to shape, guide, measure, and report the value created through business objectives, initiatives, and performance. Measuring and reporting on these goals enable business organizations to contribute to the SDGs while capitalizing on a range of benefits, (as explained later in this chapter), such as identifying future business opportunities and strengthening stakeholder engagement.

Within this context, international bodies and global initiatives have encouraged organizations to develop new instruments for providing stakeholders with a broad range of information about the impact of business strategies on sustainability. The result of this "movement" can be seen in the way sustainability has flourished and by how integrated reports have been presented by companies that have voluntarily disclosed on various environmental, social and economic aspects of their business (Joseph, 2012; Werbach, 2009; Hopwood 2009).

The focus of this chapter is to introduce the Sustainable Development Goals as a new requirement for an organization's competitiveness, to illustrate the main content of the UN 2030 Agenda for Sustainable Development, and to shed light on the reason for the debate on sustainable development that has steadily gained relevance in recent years.

In doing so, after having introduced some of the issues that have strongly influenced a redefinition of the concept of sustainable development (Sections 2 and 3), we focus our attention on a brief review of the main concepts, steps and content of SDGs as proposed by the United Nation in 2005 (Section 4). Then, the chapter points out the main challenges of sustainable development at the organizational level, presenting the new role of organizations as the real engine for SDGs (Section 5) and some examples regarding how they are approaching SDGs in practice (Section 6). Within companies, management accountants, thanks to their expertise and their role as a bridge between accounting and finance, can help foster SDGs, as discussed in Section 5. The chapter ends with some reflections on the challenges that are ahead for sustainable development issues, as well as for integrated thinking and reporting (Section 6).

3.2. Redefining sustainable growth

The set of corporate responsibilities has been changing significantly in recent years. The concept of value creation has been enlarged and replaced by the process of shared value creation (Porter and Kramer, 2011), and the meaning of sustainable development has been extended to embrace not only environmental aspects but also social inclusion and economic development.

Generally speaking, the concept of sustainable development is grounded in the so-called triple bottom line (TBL) approach (Elkington, 1994). TBL aims to broaden the focus on the financial bottom line of a business to include social and environmental responsibilities by incorporating three different dimensions of performance: social, environmental and financial. Now, societies all over the world have peacefully recognized that they have the responsibility to work for a combination of economic development, environmental sustainability and social inclusion, even if different trade-offs, synergies and objectives may arise in relation to and because of these elements.

Overcoming some attempts to compartmentalize the concept of sustainability, Drexhage and Murphy (2010, p. 20) clearly state that there is a need to get "sustainable development out of the environment "box" and considering wider social, economic, and geopolitical agendas". This is because "sustainable development embodies integrating, understanding and acting on the complex interconnections that exist between the environment, economy, and society".

In line with the above, scholars (see, among others, Joseph 2012 and Drexhage and Murphy, 2010), policymakers, standard-setters (IIRC, 2013; GRI, 2013) and organizations all over the world are looking at the concept of sustainable development with renewed interest, recognizing the urgency of the topic.

The main elements that are feeding this discussion are two: the limits of sustainability and the role of organizations.

As emphasised by Gray (2010), at the moment it is simply not possible to construct a fully reliable definition of sustainability at the corporate level because of three main reasons: (a) sustainability is a concept that can't be bounded within the corporate and organizational dimension; (b) sustainability refers to a state that can be reached in a number of ways and there is not a single sustainable position; (c) this state is the result of interactions between different actors, and it represents the net effect of these relations. Consequently, it is not necessary to require that all entities be sustainable, as possible compensations can affect the final balance.

This makes the role of organizations an issue of paramount importance, as they can mediate the reasons of capitalism with the exigencies of sustainability.

Interestingly enough, on one hand corporations have been identified as the main source of irresponsibility, to the detriment of ecological and social welfare (Bakan, 2004). The recent financial crisis and the decline of trust in the globalization model are examples of this trend.

On the other hand, due to the interactions previously mentioned, any attempt made to achieve sustainability must involve organizations, since no other solutions are feasible (Hawken *et al.,* 1999).

This situation has clearly raised a conundrum that is difficult to fix, which has put sustainability under the spotlight. In this sense, corporate sustainability reporting can be a powerful tool for measuring the contribution of a business towards the SDGs, but only if companies move from single-issue financial reporting to reporting that includes social, environmental and other sustainability factors. Adopting a multi-stakeholder approach can benefit both companies (at a corporate level) and the community (at a global level) by ensuring coherence between financial, economic, social and environmental policies.

Along this line, SDGs research has gained saliency (Schaltegger *et al.,* 2017; Bebbington and Unerman, 2018; Bebbintgton *et al.,* 2017) as companies and scholars are even more convinced that SDGs provide both an opportunity and a need for re-thinking their approach and contribution to sustainable value creation.

Moreover, government action alone cannot be sufficient for effectively achieving the SDGs target. Therefore, a concerted intervention of governments, organizations (public and private), as well as civil society and citizens is pivotal.

Within this context, there are some interesting questions to address; a few among many others are as follows: What role do organizations play in achieving sustainability – not at a corporate level – but rather at a global level? Could organizations themselves contribute to sustainable development goals in order to reduce the disruptive effects of capitalism? Is it possible to reconcile financial stability with social and environmental sustainability? And if so, how can this outcome be reached?

To answer these questions the first step is to overcome the traditional dichotomy between social, environmental, and financial concerns (see Boyd *et al.*, 2009; Orlitsky *et al.*, 2003), by adopting an integrated approach toward sustainability that goes beyond individualism in favour of a holistic view of sustainability itself.

Generally speaking, sustainable and financial performances are, by their nature, potentially in conflict and may create inherent tensions. Pursuing sustainable performance aims at creating value for society as a whole, while financial performance presents a selfish dimension that very often puts companies in conflict with social needs (Pache and Santos, 2011). Within this debate, several studies have emphasized both the advantages and disadvantages that sustainable practices can entail, such as production efficiency, cost reduction and market reputation (Miles and Covin, 2000; Ambec and Lanoie, 2008). On the contrary, the pursuit of social performance can require an increase in the costs of compliance (Jaffe *et al.*, 1995) as well as specific investments and policies that are potentially in contrast with financial performance (Hull and Rothenberg, 2008).

Within this context, the role played by SDGs within organizations appears even more challenging. Sustainable development (and sustainable development goals), in fact, cannot be achieved through isolated tactics or initiatives, but instead various actors (organizations, states, societies and individuals) must cooperate and integrate their efforts.

Finally, a common view (or trajectory) is required in order to create a sustainable system in which different actors contribute in different ways to the same goals.

3.3. The road toward Sustainable Development Goals

For the past 30 years or so, world leaders, supranational organizations, and national governments, as well as businesses and civil society, have embraced sustainability as the cornerstone in their search for development and long-term growth.

Sustainable development, conceptualized as the means for achieving sustainability, was first defined in 1987 by the United Nations' Brundtland Report as "development that meets the needs of the present without compromising the ability of future generations to meet their own needs." Also known as Our Common Future, the report was the outcome of work by the World Commission on Environment and Development (WECD, 1987), which was sponsored by the U.N. and chaired by Norwegian Prime Minister Gro Harlem Brundtland.

In the years following the release of the Brundtland Report, various institutions and international bodies have further attempted to identify the core elements of sustainable development. With the intention to address the numerous issues broadly referred to as the domain of sustainable development (such as water emergencies, health, climate change, pollution, social inequalities, access to energy, extreme poverty, and hunger), several major events and initiatives have taken place globally.

In 1992, the Rio Summit laid the foundations for the global institutionalization of sustainable development, proposing the Agenda 21 that set out actions in regard to the social and economic dimensions of sustainable development, conservation and management of natural resources, the role of major groups, and the means of implementation. Based on these premises, and according to Agenda 21 recommendations, in the same year the UN General Assembly officially created the Commission on Sustainable Development (CSD).

In September 2000, the United Nations Millennium Declaration was adopted. The Declaration committed nations to a new global partnership to reduce extreme poverty, and also set out a series of eight time-bound targets to reach by 2015, known as the Millennium Development Goals (MDGs). According to McArthur (2014)they were "the "world's first explicit development partnership framework between developed and developing countries" (p. 20).

The eight goals included: halving extreme poverty, halting the spread of HIV/AIDS, providing universal primary education, eliminating gender disparity in education, reducing the under-five mortality rate, reducing the maternal mortality rate and achieving universal access to reproductive health, developing a global partnership (to address the needs of the poorest countries, to further an open non-discriminatory trade system and to deal with developing country debt); and ensuring environmental sustainably (by integrating sustainable development into country policies and programs, reducing biodiversity loss, improving access to safe drinking water and sanitation, and improving the lives of slum dwellers) (UN, 2010).

In particular, between 2000 and 2015 the MDGs provided an important development framework producing results in several areas such as reducing poverty and improving health and education in developing countries.

According to the final MDG Report, the 15-year effort has produced the most successful anti-poverty movement in history:

- since 1990, the number of people living in extreme poverty has declined by more than half;
- the proportion of undernourished people in developing regions has fallen by almost half;
- the primary school enrolment rate in developing regions has reached 91 percent, and many more girls are now in school in comparison to the previous 15 years;
- remarkable gains have also been made in the fight against HIV/AIDS, malaria and tuberculosis;
- the under-five mortality rate has declined by more than half, and maternal mortality is down 45 percent worldwide;
- the target cut in half the number of people who lack access to improved sources of water was also met.

In 2002 at the Johannesburg World Summit, sustainable development was defined as embracing social inclusion and economic development, including environmental aspects.

In 2012, the United Nations further refined the concept of sustainable development (UN, 2012) and in 2013 the United Nations Sustainable Development Solution Network (UNSDSN) enlarged the term to include good governance as a fourth pillar. In parallel, public, private, and nongovernmental organizations have been directly involved in an attempt to coordinate efforts regarding the sustainability agenda (see, e.g., the U.N. General Assembly resolution in 2010, "United Nations Millennium Declaration-General Assembly Resolution A/RES/55/2").

This process was consolidated in 2015 when the U.N. General Assembly adopted the 2030 Agenda for Sustainable Development: a plan of action presenting a list of Sustainable Development Goals (17 objectives and 169 targets) that all countries of the world are encouraged to achieve by 2030[1]. The main purpose of the U.N. resolution is to take the steps that are urgently needed to shift the world to a more sustainable and resilient path. To achieve this target over the next fifteen years, countries will mobilize efforts to end all forms of poverty, fight inequalities and tackle climate change, while ensuring that no one is left behind.

---

[1] www.un.org/sustainabledevelopment.

The SDGs, also known as Global Goals, build on the results of the Millennium Development Goals (MDGs) and aim to go further to end all forms of poverty. In fact, according to the Resolution adopted by the General Assembly on September 2015, SDGs seek to build on the Millennium Development Goals and complete what they did not manage to achieve.

The U.N. decided to expand the goals to make them much broader, encompassing both developed and developing countries, (while the MDGs targeted mainly poor countries, the SDGs intend to define the effort required of all countries for the global well-being of this and future generations and are not just the responsibility of rich countries toward poor countries), furthermore, it expanded the challenges that must be addressed by embracing a wide range of interconnected topics across the economic, social, and environmental dimensions of sustainable development. This led to the identification and release of the SDGs, which were created by an inclusive process reflecting substantive input from all sectors of society and all parts of the world. While the MDGs focused on the poorest countries, the SDGs engage all nations in a shared, universal agenda, addressing environmental sustainability as a fundamental pillar of global wellbeing, in addition to the two pillars prioritized by the MDGs: prosperity and inclusion.

As correctly noticed by Bebbington and Unerman (2018), "one defining difference between SDGs and MDGs is the opening up of MDG Goal 7 into more detailed elements (namely: water, energy, climate change, oceans and terrestrial ecosystems), reflecting the functioning of the biosphere and its contribution to human development" (p. 4).

In this sense, governments are required to translate SDGs into national action plans, policies, and initiatives that reflect the different realities and capacities that their countries possess. While the new goals are not legally binding, governments are expected to take ownership and establish national frameworks for the achievement of the 17 Goals. Countries have the primary responsibility to follow-up and review the progress made in implementing the Goals, which will require timely, accessible and quality data collection. Regional follow-up and review will be based on national-level analyses and contribute to follow-up and review at the global level.

Differently from the MDGs, the SDGs are designed to engage a wide range of organizations and shape priorities and aspirations for sustainable development efforts around a common framework. Most importantly, the SDGs recognize the key role that business organizations can play in achieving them. Organizations, then, can be considered as being active instruments for the widespread adoption of sustainable development as a guiding principle in any aspect of business. This effort is a prerequisite for sustainable development to have any chance for real, lasting success.

Exhibit 3.1. From Sustainability to Sustainable Development.

1987	The United Nations' **Brundtland Report** provides one of the most popular definitions of sustainable development: "development that meets the needs of the present without compromising the ability of future generations to meet their own needs."
1997	The **GRI (Global Reporting Initiative)** is formed by the United States-based nonprofits Ceres (formerly the Coalition for Environmentally Responsible Economies) and Tellus Institute with the support of the United Nations Environment Programme (UNEP).
2000	The U.N. General Assembly adopts the **Millennium Declaration**. The Declaration committed nations to a new global partnership to reduce extreme poverty, and set out a series of eight time-bound targets - with a deadline of 2015 - that have become known as the Millennium Development Goals (MDGs).
2002	The **World Summit in Johannesburg** extends the definition of "sustainable development" to embrace not only environmental aspects but also social inclusion and economic development.
2011	The **Sustainability Accounting Standards Board (SASB)** is created to develop and disseminate sustainability accounting standards.
2013	The **International Integrated Reporting Council (IIRC)** releases its framework based on the concept of multicapitals to support the integration of financial and pre-financial data.
2015	The U.N. General Assembly adopts the **2030 Agenda for Sustainable Development**, accompanied by a list of Sustainable Development Goals (SDGs), namely, 17 objectives and 169 targets.

3.4. The Sustainable Development Goals

The 2030 Agenda for Sustainable Development aims at stimulating action in areas of critical importance for humanity and the planet, encompassing three dimensions: economic, social and environmental, in a balanced and integrated manner, recognizing that a change in the approach is required. In fact, until now sustainable development has been compartmentalized as an environmental issue, but the process of redefining sustainable growth, as illustrated previously, has enlarged its meaning.

In this sense, SDGs present the challenge of mobilizing action that will promote the three pillars of sustainable development at the same time.

Although the goals are not mandatory, they are acknowledged as a requirement for a competitive and globalized approach toward sustainable development. Through SDGs promoted by the United Nations, countries all over the world are stimulated to act by following an inclusive process based on the Sustainable Development Goals (see Exhibit 3.2).

Exhibit 3.2. The Sustainable Development Goals.

Goal 1   End poverty in all its forms everywhere.

Goal 2   End hunger, achieve food security and improved nutrition and promote sustainability agriculture.

Goal 3   Ensure healthy lives and promote well-being for all, at all ages.

Goal 4   Ensure inclusive and equitable quality education and promote lifelong learning opportunities for all.

Goal 5   Achieve gender equality and empower all women and girls.

Goal 6   Ensure availability and sustainable management of water and sanitation for all.

Goal 7   Ensure access to affordable, reliable, sustainable and modern energy for all.

Goal 8   Promote sustained, inclusive and sustainable economic growth, full and productive employment and decent work for all.

Goal 9   Build resilient infrastructure, promote inclusive and sustainable industrialization and foster innovation.

Goal 10   Reduce inequality within and among countries.

Goal 11   Make cities and human settlements inclusive, safe, resilient and sustainable.

Goal 12   Ensure sustainable consumption and production patterns.

Goal 13   Take urgent action to combat climate change and its impacts.

Goal 14   Conserve and sustainably use the oceans, seas and marine resources for sustainable development.

Goal 15   Protect, restore and promote sustainable use of terrestrial ecosystems, sustainably manage forests, combat desertification, and halt and reverse land degradation and halt biodiversity loss.

Goal 16   Promote peaceful and inclusive societies for sustainable development, provide access to justice for all and build effective, accountable and inclusive institutions at all levels.

Goal 17   Strengthen the means of implementation and revitalize the Global Partnership for Sustainable Development.

Source: Resolution adopted by the General Assembly on 25 September 2015. Transforming our world: the 2030 Agenda for Sustainable Development, p. 14.

Goal 1 focuses on ending poverty through interrelated strategies, including the promotion of social protection systems, decent employment and building the resilience of the poor. It represents the very essence of sustainable development. Progress has certainly been made on the global rate of extreme poverty – reduced by more than half in the last 17 years – but it is still pervasive in many regions and disproportionately affects the young.

The actions to be adopted concern the reinforcement of social protection systems, the increase of decent work opportunities and the strengthening of disaster risk reduction.

Goal 2 addresses a fundamental human need: access to nutritious, healthy food, and the means by which it can be sustainably secured for everyone. The solution for this enormous problem can't be simply by increasing food production. The intervention must refer to system changes, such as well-functioning markets, increased incomes for smallholder farmers, equal access to technology and land, and additional investments in the agricultural sector.

Investing in agriculture is widely recognized as one of the most effective means to alleviate poverty, improve food security and reduce hunger and malnutrition. However, UN official data reveal an alarming situation. The share of aid to agriculture from member countries of the Development Assistance Committee of the Organization for Economic Co-operation and Development (OECD-DAC) has fallen from nearly 20 percent in the mid-1980s to only 7 percent in 2015, reflecting a shift away from the financing of infrastructure and production towards a greater focus on social sectors.

Goal 3 addresses all major health priorities and calls for improving reproductive, maternal and child health; ending communicable diseases; reducing non-communicable diseases and other health hazards; and ensuring universal access to safe, effective, quality and affordable medicines and vaccines, as well as health coverage.

Goal 4 aims to ensure that all people have access to quality education and an opportunity for lifelong learning. The Goal goes beyond school enrolment and looks at proficiency levels, the availability of trained teachers and adequate school facilities and disparities in education outcomes.

This goal is evidently impacted by educational systems that are struggling to keep up with population growth and have serious problems with the quality of the education offered (if any). The situation is even more critical if we consider vulnerable populations, specifically the disabled, indigenous people, rural poor or refugees.

Goal 5 refers to gender inequality. Women's empowerment and gender equality are conditions strictly linked and interconnected with Goals 3 and 4. Significant progress can be obtained only by increasing female enrolment at all education levels, reducing maternal mortality and increasing skilled care. Obviously, achieving gender equality and the empowerment of women and girls will require vigorous action that includes strong interventions in various legal frameworks and a strong fight against discrimination, which is too often derived from social norms.

Goal 6 aims to tackle challenges related to drinking water, sanitation and hygiene for populations, as well as to water-related ecosystems. These conditions are prerequisites for progress in many other areas across the SDGs including health, education and poverty reduction. In addition, the right use and protection of water are critical for the economic system, for producing food and for all productive sectors.

Goal 7 refers to universal access to affordable, reliable and sustainable energy services. Achieving this goal requires expanding access to electricity and clean cooking fuels and technologies, as well as improving energy efficiency and increasing the use of renewable energy. As more than 3 billion people still lack access to clean cooking fuels and technologies, bolder financing and policies will be needed, along with the willingness of countries to embrace innovative technologies on a much more ambitious scale.

Goal 8 focuses on an element that can theoretically act as both a driver or an obstacle for sustainable development. In fact, economic growth is a principal driver of sustainable development if it is sustainable and inclusive, and more people can escape poverty as opportunities for full and productive employment expand. At the same time, economic growth can be boosted to the detriment of people and resources. When countries are depleting their natural resources for the sake of economic growth, they are creating damage that will have an effect on future generations and reduce the sustainable development of the country itself. To allow future generations to benefit from today's economic growth, such growth should be environmentally sound and not the result of an unsustainable exploitation of resources. Indicators adopted in the evaluation of the results connected to Goal 8 are: high real economic growth; growth in labour productivity; youth unemployment; child labour and access to financial services.

Goal 9 assumes that infrastructure, industrialization and innovation are the three main driving forces for economic growth and sustainable development. They can help countries in reducing poverty by creating new job opportunities, stimulating growth and encouraging the building and improvement of physical facilities that are essential for the functioning of business and society (and for the achievement of the previous goals).

Goal 10 calls for reducing inequality within and among countries, ensuring safe, orderly and regular migration, and strengthening the voices of developing countries in international economic and financial decision making. The results of these actions are already visible and between 2010 and 2015 the income and/or consumption of the bottom 40 percent of the population grew faster than the national average in 49 of the 83 countries included in the data.

Goal 11 aims to make cities and human settlements inclusive, safe, resilient and sustainable. It recognizes that rapid urbanization has brought with it enormous challenges, including inadequate housing, increased air pollution and a lack of access to basic services and infrastructure. In 2015, 54 percent of the world's population lived in cities, which had serious consequences on waste management, pollution, problems in urban planning and housing, to mention only a few.

Goal 12 defines sustainable consumption and production patterns as being factors that enable efficient resource use and that can reduce the impact of economic activities on the environment. The goal is dramatically impacted by the material footprints of human beings. The material footprint is defined as the amount of raw material extracted globally to meet the consumption demand of a country. Achieving this goal requires strong national frameworks for sustainable consumption and production that are integrated into national and sectorial plans, along with sustainable business practices and consumer behaviour.

Goal 13 responds to planetary warming, requiring urgent actions to combat climate change and its impacts. Meeting this goal will require building on the momentum achieved by the Paris Agreement on Climate Change. The changes we are witnessing are affecting people everywhere, but they disproportionately harm the poorest and the most vulnerable. Stronger efforts are also needed to build resilience and limit climate-related hazards and natural disasters.

Goal 14 sets an action plan to conserve and sustainably use the oceans, seas and marine resources for sustainable development. Oceans cover almost three-quarters of the planet, comprising the largest ecosystem on Earth. The increasingly adverse impact of climate change (including ocean acidification), overfishing and marine pollution are jeopardizing recent gains in protecting portions of the world's oceans.

Goal 15 refers to the protection, restoration and promotion of the sustainable use of terrestrial ecosystems. To meet this goal, it is necessary to sustainably manage forests, combat desertification, halt and reverse land degradation and halt biodiversity loss. Protecting and restoring ecosystems and the biodiversity they support can help mitigate climate change and provide increased resilience in the face of mounting human pressures and natural disasters. Healthy ecosystems also produce multiple benefits for the communities that rely on them. Goal 15 focuses on preserving and sustainably using the Earth's terrestrial species and ecosystems.

Goal 16 defines what could be perhaps be defined as the core of sustainable development. It focuses on the promotion of peaceful and inclusive societies for sustainable development, the access to justice for all and the creation of effective, accountable and inclusive institutions at all levels. Peace, justice and effective, accountable and inclusive institutions are at the core of sustainable development. Progress in promoting peaceful and inclusive societies remains uneven across and within countries. Violent conflicts have increased in recent years and a number of high-intensity armed conflicts are causing large numbers of civilian casualties and driving millions of people from their homes.

Goal 17 clearly outlines that a stronger commitment to partnership and cooperation is needed to achieve sustainable development at a global level. Attaining the goals will require coherent policies, an enabling environment for sustainable development at all levels and by all actors, and a reinvigorated Global Partnership for Sustainable Development. Therefore, the critical issues are the following: resource mobilization, technology, capacity-building, trade, policy and institutional coherence, multi-stakeholder partnerships, and data monitoring and accountability.

3.5. A new role for organizations

As discussed above, the goal of sustainable development is not feasible without an active engagement of organizations (Hawken *et al.,* 1999).

Being sustainable and attempting to achieve the SDGs is a strategy that is increasingly being made by proactive and sustainable organizations. In so doing, making SDG alignment part of their strategies and business models can help companies generate new revenue, increase supply chain resilience, recruit and retain talent, spawn investor interest, and assure license to operate.

According to PWC (2015), SDG awareness amongst the business community is high (92% of the total group surveyed), while the exact nature and requirements of the SDGs are not yet common knowledge among citizens (33%). The results of the survey, then, shows a significant gap in awareness, but organizations are taking action and nearly 71% of the business participants surveyed are already making plans on how to respond to SDGs and engage with them.

These business organizations want to achieve the same ends as any other company by driving revenue growth, creating value, and accelerating business expansion. However, critically contributing to the SDGs through inclusive business models helps these organizations reinforce their awareness of the multiple and heterogeneous resources they use, as well as the impact of the company's activities on stakeholders.

In order to leverage these advantages, the integration between sustainability initiatives and business goals should be comprehensive. Numerous successful companies have adopted this approach, steadily growing their bottom lines through innovation and adaptation while simultaneously stimulating progress toward the SDGs. This is because they have recognized the opportunities inherent in developing and delivering solutions for the achievement of the SDGs, which can simultaneously act as opportunities for new growth and also as a means of reducing their risk profile.

For example, a pharmaceutical company[2] investing in R&D and using its knowledge, money and expertise to find new ways to positively impact public health, may contribute to the achievement of Goal 3 (Good health and wellbeing).

Automotive companies[3] investing in e-mobility, electric and hybrid transportation, safety and innovation contribute to the achievement of Goal 3 (Good health and wellbeing), Goal 12 (responsible consumption and production), Goal 7 (affordable and clean energy), Goal 11 (sustainable cities and communities) and Goal 13 (climate action), by integrating sustainability initiatives and business goals.

Organizations within the fashion industry[4] that decide to raise the bar on traceability and animal welfare or to promote sustainable design and to minimize the environmental impact of a product at every stage, from sourcing and manufacturing to transportation and consumer use, contribute to Goal 12 (responsible consumption and production), Goal 13 (climate action) and Goal 15 (life on land).

Moreover, improving diversity in the workforce can positively impact Goal 5 (gender equality). Re-engineering the lifecycle of products or the entire production cycle can contribute by reducing the carbon footprint. Increasing energy efficiency and decreasing dependence on limited resources and reducing waste can produce evident effects on Goal 12 (responsible consumption and production), Goal 7 (affordable and clean energy) and Goal 13 (climate action).

The links and the patterns depicted above highlight how organizations can leverage SDGs with the purpose of enabling value creation processes (at a company level) and contributing to sustainable development at a global level.

In this scenario, PWC (2015) affirms that it is quite clear where business sees its contribution, depicting both business impact on the SDGs and the potential opportunities (see Exhibit 3.3).

Recognizing their role into the business cycle, companies ranked SDG 8 (Decent work and economic growth) as the top SDG they have the greatest impact on and as offering them the greatest business opportunity.

The balance between impact and opportunities is obviously driven by the companies' industry sector (see chapter 5 on this point). It's hardly surprising that companies in the Energy, Utilities and Mining sector say they

---

[2] https://www.pfizer.com/files/investors/financial_reports/annual_reports/2016/our-business/sustainable -development-goals-sdgs/index.html.

[3] https://www.daimler.com/sustainability/.

[4] http://www.kering.com/en/press-releases/kering_signals_a_new_path_for_luxury_with_the_launch_of_its_next_generation;https://www.stellamccartney.com/experience/it/ pressroom/stella-mccartney-converts-to-tipa-sustainable-packaging-solutions/.

have the greatest impact on SDG 7 (Affordable and clean energy); the Healthcare sector highlights SDG 3 (Good health and wellbeing), while the Chemical sector cites SDG 13 (Climate action).

It's interesting to note that PWC (2015) analyses the previous results also in relation to the geographical area, highlighting that globally, all regions listed SDG 8 (Decent work and economic growth) as the SDG where they could have the most impact apart from the Middle East where companies identified SDG 3 (Good health and well-being) as the most pressing goal.

Exhibit 3.3. Business impact on the SDGs and potential opportunities.

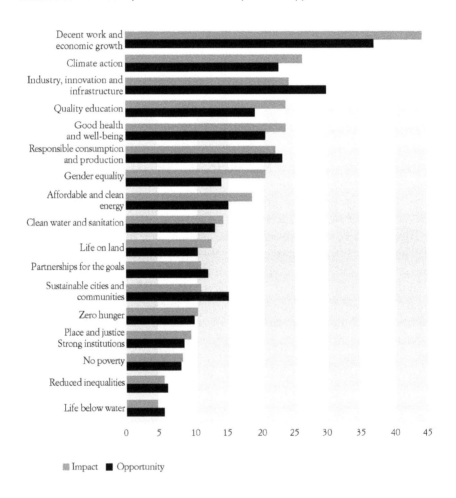

Source: PwC, 2015, p. 10.

If we consider the possible benefits of sustainability from the company perspective, different authors have argued that effective environmental management may lead to increased production efficiency, cost reduction and improved market reputation with benefits for financial performance (see Molina-Azorín *et al.*, 2009; Ambec and Lanoie, 2008; Miles and Covin, 2000).

The GRI, the United Nations and the WBCSD (2017:8) define a series of benefits, summarized in Exhibit 3.3, that companies can obtain by developing and delivering solutions in order to achieve SDGs:

- Identifying future business opportunities;
- Enhancing the value of corporate sustainability;
- Strengthening stakeholder relations and keeping pace with policy developments;
- Stabilizing societies and markets;
- Using a common language and shared purpose.

A green and sustainable economy is already a reality in which a number of companies are investing, re-focusing their business model and delivering innovative and effective solutions that, on one hand, enrich the business portfolio (and hopefully financial results), and on the other hand aim to improve human well-being and social equity, and reduce environmental risks and ecological scarcities.

The SDG's purpose is to boost this trend, fostering a new awareness and redirecting public and private investments toward innovative business opportunities such as advanced technologies that allow an increase in energy efficiency, energy storage and the use of renewable energy or new solutions for sustainable transportation and 'green buildings'. Other market opportunities that SDGs can offer refer to changes in the traditional manufacturing process in favour of advanced technology solutions that reduce emissions and waste, or to the discovery of new markets that are at the moment untapped, offering products and services to people who currently live in poverty.

Delivering SDGs can positively impact the financial value drivers of corporate sustainability such as market reputation, employees' engagement and productivity and reduction of risk. Moreover, such efforts can help companies attract capitals for socially responsible investors or ethical funds.

Exhibit 3.4. Benefits of SDGs.

The global commitment to deliver the SDGs will further strengthen the relations between companies and stakeholders. This because developing and delivering solutions for the achievement of SDGs permits an improvement in relations with regulators and stakeholders in general, creates stronger relationships with communities, and attains lower compliance costs. Successful implementation of the SDGs will help to enhance legitimacy in terms of improved credibility with the public, reduced litigation and reduced future liability for environmental damage.

Consequently, the interaction between organizations, individuals, and states can lead to the stabilization of societies and markets that could undoubtedly favour business at all levels.

As highlighted by the GRI, the United Nations and the WBCSD (2017:9), the implementation of the SDGs will help to:

• "lift billions of people out of poverty, thereby growing consumer markets around the world;

• strengthen education, thereby fostering more skilled and engaged employees;

• make progress on gender equality and women empowerment, thereby creating a 'virtual emerging market' equivalent in size and purchasing power to that of China's and India's populations;

• ensure that the global economy operates safely within the capacity of the planet to supply essential resources such as water, fertile soil, metals and minerals, thereby sustaining the natural resources that companies depend on for production;

• foster accountable and well-governed institutions as well as open and rule-based trading and financial systems, thereby reducing the costs and risks of doing business".

Finally, the SDGs enable the definition of a set of priorities and purposes across the different dimensions of sustainable development that companies share all over the world, which means that business will be using a unique, common language and a shared purpose.

This can facilitate the communication process (and comparability among different entities) regarding performances and impacts, consequently helping companies to offer consistent and effective information to stakeholders. Thus, SDGs become the tool companies can leverage to inform stakeholders about which activities are generating wealth and what instruments the organisation is using to exploit them.

3.6. How companies make SDGs happen: cases and best practices.

In order to make SDGs happen and to exploit the benefits listed above, companies' journey toward effective sustainable development should have some important characteristics.

Firstly, a complete assessment of companies' priorities has to be addressed and a scan of the impacts that business activities have on the SDGs is required. In particular, both current and potential future impacts are relevant in this phase. Examining the value chain and mapping the high impact areas allow companies to define priorities across the SDGs. This implies that a context analysis also has to be developed, including considerations on the likelihood that new regulation, standardization, market, labour or materials shortage, and stakeholder pressure modify the scenario analysed.

Secondly, companies should identify and list goals that help foster shared priorities and improve performance. In order to be effective, these goals should be clear and understandable and must cover all the priorities previously defined across the dimensions of a triple bottom line: the economic, social and environmental aspects of sustainable development. The more these goals are specific, measurable and time-bound, the more they will also drive good performance.

Coherent with the SDG approach and the global responsibility of companies, even this phase of goal settings is, in a certain sense, externally driven. By adopting an outside-in approach, companies are required to prioritize goals in accordance to what is needed externally from a global perspective. As a result, they can gain recognition from the outside, engage business partners and external stakeholders who are particularly interested in sustainable development issues.

Thirdly, in order to correctly address the goals that have been set and the strategic priorities, companies should integrate sustainability into their core business and embed targets across functions. Depending on the nature and the history of the companies, this task can vary and present some difficulties in its implementation, but a truly effective integration can lead to a series of advantages. The integration of SDGs in the business model can positively influence many aspects of companies' core business, including the products and services offered, customer segments, R&D function, supply chain management, use of materials and distribution networks, as well as strategy and communication.

Finally, all the previous phases should be reported and communicated to stakeholders. In fact, companies should provide any information that enables stakeholders to clearly understand how strategy is aligned with sustainable development, thus connecting business with global priorities. This practice is even more important in cases in which companies have (correctly) set their goals in accordance with stakeholders' needs. In this case, the regular reporting of performance and targets, in other terms, will inform stakeholders about the company's ability to meet their needs and expectations.

What is particularly relevant here is that the SDGs make this level of communication and reporting a clear expectation for markets and stakeholders in general. The SDG target 12.6, i.e., calls on governments to "encourage companies, especially large and trans-national companies, to adopt sustainable practices and to integrate sustainability information into their reporting cycle".

In light of the above, this section aims to shed light on the early experiences of some companies that are active in different sectors, to illustrate their attempt to achieve SDGs, integrate sustainability in strategy and processes, set goals and report and communicate these efforts. Ultimately, the examples demonstrate how business growth and socioeconomic development can thrive together.

In particular, the cases presented here refer to Iberdrola and Electrolux, two multinational companies that, conscious of their role in society, have linked their outcomes and strategy to the SDGs, defining priorities and impacts.

3.6.1. Iberdrola: the alignment between strategy and the SDGs

Iberdrola is one of the leading electric companies in the world, mainly active in five countries of the Atlantic area (Spain, the United Kingdom, the United States, Mexico and Brazil). In 2006, the company earned 29 million euros, with 7.8 million euros as EBITDA. As of December 31, 2016, its installed capacity was 46,926 MW, with 27,723 MW of renewable installed capacity. The company employees totalled 30,591, serving 34.5 million users.

Its attention toward sustainable development is declared in its mission "to create value in a sustainable way and commit to social dividend". Therefore, the company is particularly focused on using environmentally friendly energy sources and investing in innovation to fight against climate change through all of its business activities.

Along these lines, it has launched a number of initiatives – such as the Sustainability Scorecard, the International Start-up Program, the Sustainable Mobility Plan, and the Corporate International Volunteering Programme, to mention some – that aim to show its contribution to sustainable development.

Iberdrola put in place a strong sustainability commitment as the foundation of its mission. Along this line, the Sustainability Scorecard represents a tool for evaluating the Group's sustainability performance by analysing its economic, environmental and social dimensions. It is used to determine which aspects require improvement throughout the Group as a whole and can be interpreted as a means of prioritizing the sustainable strategy to pursue. The main result of this assessment obviously supports the company in mapping the high impact areas related to SDGs. In this sense, this analysis has reinforced the centrality of clean energy need for Iberdrola's business model. The outlook for the future is for strong growth in world energy demand that must be satisfied with clean and efficient technologies to meet the global pledge to reduce emissions. The company is, therefore, aware that the electricity sector plays a key role in tackling these challenges efficiently, thanks to its technological potential for contributing to the decarbonisation of the economy, thanks to renewable energies. With its commitment to a model of sustainable energy, Iberdrola has been at the forefront of the energy transition with its support for the sustainable solutions required by the increasing electrification of the world economy: more clean energies, more storage capacity, more backup energy, more and more intelligent grids, and greater digitisation.

The International Start-up Program focuses on technologies and business models that can improve the sustainability of the energy model through a higher degree of electrification and the decarbonisation of the economy. The objectives of the program echo some of the SDGs integration into companies' strategy depicted in paragraph 5. Thanks to this, in fact, Iberdrola intends to (a) identify early the key trend for the future of the company; (b) access ground-breaking technologies and business models and (c) foster a culture of innovation and entrepreneurial activity.

Finally, while presenting the Sustainable Mobility Plan and the Corporate International Volunteering Programme, Iberdrola immediately links the two initiatives with SDGs. The former intends to supply affordable and clean energy (Goal 7), in line with actions to combat climate change (Goal 13), promoting efficient and responsible energy use and a sustainable and smart mobility system. In addition, it contributes directly to achieving Goals 13 (action for the climate) and 11 (sustainable cities and communities), and indirectly to Goals 3 (health and well-being), 8 (decent work and economic growth) and 9 (industry, innovation and infrastructure).

The Corporate International Volunteering Programme, instead, recognizes Goals 7, 13, 3, 4 and 10 as the main targets for its implementation.

According to the Iberdrola Integrated Report for 2017 (p. 30), the Spanish company has completely incorporated the Sustainable Development Goals into its business strategy and its Sustainability Policy.

As shown in its Integrated Reporting for 2017, Iberdrola has centred its business model on the supply of reliable, high-quality and environmental-friendly energy, clearly stating that it wants to be a "responsible and sustainable company, serving society and people". The report suggests how the company can and wishes to play a pivotal role in sustainable development over the long term by balancing its financial goals with local socioeconomic growth.

In 2016, PricewaterhouseCoopers released a study on Iberdrola's impact on society (based on figures from 2015), focusing on the economic, social, and environmental aspects for the countries in which it does business.

The main results reveal:

- annual generation of more than 27,000 million euros in Gross Domestic Product (GDP) in the countries in which it operates;
- annual contribution of more than 4,400 million euros in investments, for the capital formation of the world economy;
- investment of more than 2,300 million euros in the "green generation" (2013-2015), entailing:
  - installed green capacity (hydroelectric and renewable) constituting 55% of all of Iberdrola's installed capacity;
  - avoidance of the emission of more than 57 million tonnes of CO_2;
- creation of close to 300,000 jobs throughout the world (direct, indirect, and induced employment);
- investments of more than 100 million euros in rural electrification programs in Brazil (2013-2015), and facilitating access to electricity for more than 1.4 million people in developing countries (2014-2015).

From this data, the relevance of such activities in terms of sustainability, at a macro-level is clear. This has led Iberdrola to measure its achievements against the SDGs. The commitment to SDGs is the first chapter in the Sustainability section of the company website.

In 2016, for the first time it introduced the topic into its Integrated Report, highlighted that SDGs entail the recognition of energy as an engine of sustainable growth, and, therefore, they are relevant for the company. But at the time, they briefly discussed the goals only in relation to natural capital, in the outlook section related to the prevention of pollution. In that context, in fact, Iberdrola recognized that its intention was to actively participate in achieving the Sustainable Development Goals approved in September 2015 (Goals 6, 7, and 13).

The company's attention to SDGs received a boost in 2017 when, in the Integrated Report, Iberdrola adopted a more complete approach to SDGs disclosure, by defining:

• its commitment to SDGs, which has led the company to fully integrate them in its strategy;
• three different levels of priority, that define the contribution of Iberdrola to sustainable development (see Figure 4.5);
• the targets – for the short, medium and long term – that the company has defined in relation to the goals assumed as its principal focus.

As an electric company, in this way, Iberdrola has defined two major focuses of its activity: maximizing the access to electricity (focusing on Goal 7) and taking urgent action to combat climate change and its impact (fostering Goal 13).

First, Iberdrola plans to achieve a 30% reduction in the intensity of CO_2 emissions by 2020 (compared to those in 2007), and a 50% reduction in emissions intensity by 2030. The long-term strategy will lead the company to be carbon neutral by 2050. This path is already on-going and at the end of 2016 Iberdrola's emissions intensity was 34% lower than the European average, moreover, 66% of its installed capacity is emission-free.

Second, to offer affordable and clean energy, the company's goal, to be reached by 2020, is to bring electricity to 4 million people who today lack access to this energy source. The goal is in line with the results obtained in 2016 when the company, through projects carried out in various countries of Latin America and Africa, had contributed to providing electricity to 2.5 million people.

Exhibit 3.5. Iberdrola's prioritization of SDGs.

Source: Iberdrola Integrated Report 2017, p. 30.

In addition, the company web site offers some additional insights into Iberdrola's integration of (other) sustainable development goals into its core business. The Group recognizes, in fact, that its activity directly contributes to ensuring clean water and sanitation (Goal 6), has increased the investment in R&D&I[5] activities (Goal 9), promotes the respect for the life of land ecosystems (Goal 15) and works to create partnerships to achieve these goals (Goal 17).

As illustrated above, in the Integrated Report 2017, Iberdrola presented some key data and information about the company's contribution to SDGs.

The structure of the disclosure presented, at least in part, reflects on the steps designed by the SDG Compass for a proper measurement and management of the company's contribution to the Sustainable Development Goals.

Developed by GRI, the UN Global Compact and the World Business Council for Sustainable Development (WBSCSD), the SDG Compass intends to guide companies in aligning their strategies to SDGs, maximizing their contribution to sustainable development and allowing them to capitalize on a range of benefits.

---

[5] R&D&I stands for Research, Development and Innovation.

According to SDG Compass, the five steps a company has to respect in order to ensure sustainability as an outcome of its business model are as follows:

1. understanding the SDGs,
2. defining priorities,
3. setting goals,
4. integrating,
5. reporting and communicating.

In the case of Iberdrola, out of these 5 steps at least 2 requirements appear to be completely respected. The company clearly defines its priorities in terms of SDGs (step 2) and enlarges its discussion on the topic by distinguishing between goals that are directly impacted and indirectly impacted.

In addition, it identifies specific SDGs impact targets in the short, medium and long term (to provide electricity to a targeted number of people and to reduce CO_2 levels), consequently fulfilling step 3.

In relation to steps 4 and 5, the Iberdrola Integrated Report offers some insights into the process of integration of the SDGs into its business strategy and sustainability process; however, further analysis is required and more effective communication about sustainability strategy and performance should be added.

To seize the most important business opportunities presented by the SDGs and to reduce risks, companies need to integrate the management of sustainable development issues into everyday business decision making while assessing both the positive (or negative) and current (and potential) impacts on the SDGs across their value chains.

Goal setting, outcome measurement and performance communication are critical to business success and help to foster shared priorities and better performance across the organization.

3.6.2. Electrolux: For the Better

Electrolux is one of the main multinational companies operating in the sector of household appliances and appliances for professional use. Its most recognized brands are Electrolux, AEG, Zanussi and Frigidaire.

The company, previously known as AB Lux, was founded in 1901, and listed for the first time in 1928 on the London Stock Exchange. From 1984, Electrolux has increased its propensity towards foreign investment, first with acquisitions in Europe, and then at a worldwide level. In 1984, Italian appliance manufacturer Zanussi was acquired, making Electrolux the European leader in household appliances for consumers and professionals.

Two years later, it acquired the third largest appliance company in the U.S., White Consolidated, with brands such as Frigidaire, Kelvinator and Westinghouse. The group became even stronger in 1994, when the appliance manufacturer AEG was acquired. The growth strategy was further addressed in 2001 (with the acquisition of the household appliance division of the Australian company Email) and in 2011 (when the Olympic Group in Egypt and CTI in Chile were acquired).

Today, Electrolux is a multinational group operating in three core markets (Western Europe; North America and Australia; New Zealand and Japan) and is heavily investing in three other growth markets (Africa, Middle East and Eastern Europe; Latin America; Southeast Asia and China).

The Group boasts 60 million products sold annually, 55,400 employees, with about 12 billion Euros in sales.

In 2015, for the first time, the company recognized the planet as one of its main stakeholders, as well as its customers, employees and shareholders. In this way, the company explicitly recognized that sustainability leadership is crucial to realizing its strategy.

Later on, in early 2016, Electrolux launched the sustainability program, named *"For the Better"*, that marks a new step in the integration between sustainability and their business model.

According to the 2016 Sustainability Report, the company management wants to take Electrolux's sustainability leadership to the next level in this way, (see p. 2). Sustainability information is also integrated throughout the Annual Report. Targeted at shareholders and other stakeholders, the focus is on how sustainability issues relate to the business strategy, as well as to goals and performance.

The Electrolux Sustainability Framework – *For the Better* – covers three areas: Better Solutions, Better Operations and Better Society.

Within these areas, Electrolux defines nine promises that it presents as the springboard that will make a difference between now and 2020. These promises cover all the stages of the value chain – from R&D and suppliers, operations and consumers, to the products' end-of-life policy. The in-depth analysis of both the promises and of the results achieved, reveals how the company is pointing out its efforts in fighting climate change. In fact, due to its core business, Electrolux addresses climate change as one of the greatest, most urgent challenges to face and defines targets and strategies that it is implementing in relation to this challenge.

Interestingly enough, *For the Better* is a document that is highly used by the company to define targets in relation to a series of goals, which reveals their strong focus on the assessment of the company's impact on society. In this sense, and to present a complete picture of its activity, Electrolux sets (and reports on) both absolute goals as well as relative ones.

Absolute goals take into account only the selected KPI, as seen in the following quotation:

"We've reduced the total carbon footprint, including product use, by 27% since 2005", (p. 14); while relative (or intensity) goals compare the KPI to a unit of output, as seen here: "in 2016, our total greenhouse gas emissions per unit manufactured was half of that seen in 2005", (p. 4).

This reporting choice is significant for two main reasons.

Firstly, by using these two different types of goals, Electrolux implicitly recognizes that neither type, when taken separately, can provide a complete picture of the impact the company aims to achieve, and, as a consequence, it offers a global vision of its outcomes. Absolute goals, in fact, best express the expected impact on society but do not take company growth (or decline) into account. Relative targets, on the other hand, measure the company's performance per unit of output more accurately, but the impact the goal will have is unsure.

Secondly, Electrolux reinforces a clear statement presented in its Sustainability Framework: "ambitious targets drive performance", (p. 8). According to SDG Compass (GRI, United Nations and WBCSD, 2017:18), "ambitious goals are likely to drive greater impacts and better performance than more modest goals" and, at the same time, they can generate additional advantages not only at company level but also at system level. Ambitious targets can have reputational implications, and industry leaders create pressures on their peers to keep up. For example, if one company commits to a living wage for all employees, others in the same sector will have to follow suit or be left behind. As previously mentioned, as a consequence of this trend, leading companies have recently started to take a more 'outside-in' approach to goal setting. This process is strongly influenced by SDGs that now represent the main "external pressure factor" that can influence companies' goal setting.

With this in mind, Electrolux's 2016 Sustainability Report identifies three main goals that are particularly relevant for the Group and closely aligned with the promises on which *For the Better* has been founded.

In particular, they are (in order of relevance): Goal 12 – Responsible consumption and production; Goal 13 – Climate Action; Goal 8 – Decent work and economic growth.

Referring to Goal 12, the company is striving to bring resource-efficient products that are manufactured in a sustainable way, to as many people as possible around the world. Within this strategy, Electrolux is setting ambitious targets to reduce the carbon footprint of the products, production and also related to its suppliers.

Goal 13, then, is perfectly integrated into Electrolux's climate target of cutting in half its CO2 footprint, including product usage, production and transportation. They are committed to achieving Science Based Emission Targets and have set a new target to increase the share of renewable energy used in operations to 50%.

The first results presented in the Sustainability Report highlighted a decrease of 27% of the total carbon footprint, including product use, since 2005, and the target for 2020 will call for preventing the release of 25 million tonnes of carbon dioxide and its equivalents (CO2e) into the atmosphere over 15 years – from 2005 to 2020.

In line with these results, in 2016 Electrolux was recognised as a global leader in its response to climate change by CDP, the international not-for-profit organization that guides sustainable economies. Electrolux is among an exclusive group of companies worldwide that have been awarded a position on the CDP's Climate A List.

Exhibit 3.6. Electrolux's climate target 2020.

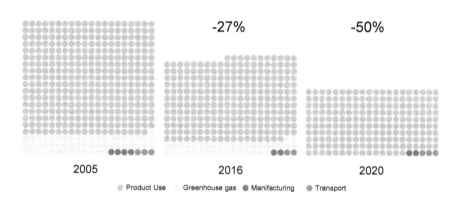

Source: Electrolux Sustainability Report 2016, p. 14.

Finally, as a priority for its strategy and growth, the company recognizes SDG number 8. Creating decent work conditions is already the basis for Electrolux' Code of Conduct, first established in 2002, which requires this principle for both the company as well as for their suppliers.

3.7. The role of management accountants in making SDGs happen

As discussed above, the integration between sustainability initiatives and business goals is currently contributing to making SDGs happen in practice. This because organizations strive to align competitiveness and sustainable growth. Thanks to their position and expertise, management accounting professionals have the potential to play a key role within this process.

Today, organizations operate in a complex and rapidly changing world, characterized by a multitude of internal and external drivers, interdependencies, and trade-offs that influence the process of decision making, the promises that these decisions entail, and the expectations of a variety of stakeholders. Within this context, most organizations strive to balance competitiveness and sustainable growth by implementing programs and initiatives of sustainability that intend to achieve specific targets in terms of governance, social and environmental impact. But isolated sustainability tactics do not guarantee the achievement of sustainable performance(s), which instead requires an integrated approach to the planning, management, and reporting that must take into consideration how the interests and the contributions of a series of heterogeneous stakeholders are linked to the models for long-term value creation. Management accounting professionals have the great opportunity to lead the process of making SDGs happen and connect performance with purpose. Because of their financial expertise and positioning with organizations, they can contribute significantly to identifying, executing, and monitoring business decisions and strategies for long-term value creation.

Management accounting offers tools and engagement platforms that can go beyond the representation of the initiatives of sustainability through a set of ad hoc targets and key performance indicators to include processes of mediation among the different stakeholders who are involved. In this area, management accountants and finance experts in general can lead the search for sustainable performance by suggesting pragmatic solutions that can monitor and communicate ways in which such an inclusive strategy, and the purpose of business models, may be converted into added value for a multitude of stakeholders.

The measurement and internal/external reporting of sustainability strategies and performance by business organizations is an important issue for management accountants and financial professionals (see Bekefi and Epstein, 2016). For internal reporting, it's critical to integrate sustainability strategies and performance in planning, decision-making, and monitoring activities. For external reporting, designing reports that are relevant and useful for a variety of stakeholders – including investors – is critical. In this sense, the attempt to connect competitiveness and sustainable growth cannot overlook the cooperation between the finance experts and the sustainability function. This has led to innovative planning, measurement, and reporting processes and practices, which have embodied inclusive strategies and business models designed to take advantage of the opportunities of the market and navigate through the challenges that such a comprehensive–but very much needed–approach presents. Overall, while making SDGs happen will be an opportunity and challenge for governments and business organizations in the years ahead, this process will rely on the skills and evolving expertise of management accounting professionals.

3.8. Summary and conclusions

The aim of this chapter was to provide a comprehensive introduction to Sustainable Development Goals, a set of goals and targets that now represents a new requirement for the competitiveness of organizations.

In this chapter we have highlighted that the SDGs have been generally recognized as an important opportunity for moving beyond the development agenda of the Millennium Development Goals (MDG) towards a universally relevant agenda that, by relying on the triple bottom line approach, integrates social, economic and environmental goals, and includes targets for both developed and developing countries.

The concept of sustainability is not new at all and it has strongly evolved over time.

In view of the limited success of environmental governance, the SDGs target not only governments, but other change agents such as businesses, citizens and civil society, by asking for an active involvement of all relevant stakeholders. In this scenario, by relying upon the evolving debate regarding sustainability and sustainable development, we have emphasised the role of organizations in promoting and realizing the SDGs.

The correct implementation of this engagement process can end in a win-win situation in which organizations actively contribute to sustainable development and, at the same time, can benefit from a series of advantages. Transitioning to more sustainable practices, in fact, represents a company's source of a long enduring competitive advantage since it can be translated into new market opportunities, better reputation, lower risk and a new boost toward innovation.

To reach these goals, the SDGs need to connect to the logic of the business and finance community, and mobilize and engage them as agents of change. This process is challenging, but companies are aware of the benefits that can be derived from integrating sustainability into strategy, such as, first-mover advantages, reduction of global supply chain risks and efficiency gains. Therefore, in this scenario, authorities and scholars recall a more relevant role of the company, which could represent the real engine of the SDGs.

In this sense, this chapter has presented two business cases that rely on the experiences of organizations that put sustainable development at the forefront of their strategy. These examples illustrate how the SDGs have been integrated into the strategic core of many leading businesses, in different sectors.

3.9. References

Ambec, S. and Lanoie P. (2008), "Does it pay to be green? A systematic overview". *Academy of Manage Perspectives*, Vo. 22 No. 4, pp. 45-62.

Bakan, J. (2004), *The corporation: the pathological pursuit of profit and power*, New York: Free Press.

Bebbington, J., Russell, S. and Thomson, I. (2017), "Accounting and sustainable development: reflections and propositions", *Critical Perspectives on Accounting*, Vol. 48, pp. 21-34.

Bebbington, J., Unerman, J. (2018), "Achieving the United Nations Sustainable Development Goals: an enabling role for accounting research", *Accounting, Auditing & Accountability Journal*, Vol. 31 No. 1, pp. 2-24.

Bekefi, T. and Epstein, M. (2016), "21st Century Sustainability", *Strategic Finance*, November, pp. 28-37.

Boyd, B., Henning, N., Reyna, E., Wang, D.E., Welch, M.D. (2009), *Hybrid organizations: new business models for environmental leadership*, Greenleaf, Sheffield.

Drexhage J., Murphy, D. (2010), *Sustainable development: from Brundtland to Rio 2012, Background paper for the high-level panel on global sustainability*, United Nations, New York. http://www.un.org/wcm/webdav/site/climatechange/shared/gsp/docs/GSP16_Background%20on%20Sustainable%20Devt.pdf.

Electrolux (2016), Sustainability Report. http://www.electroluxgroup.com/en/category/sustainability/sustainability-reports/. Accessed 15 December 2017.

Elkington, J. (1994), "Towards the Sustainable Corporation: Win-Win-Win Business Strategies for Sustainable Development", *California Management Review*, Vol. 36 No. 2, pp. 90-100.

Gray R. (2010), "Is accounting for sustainability actually accounting for sustainability... and how would we know? An exploration of narratives of organisations and the planet", *Accounting Organizations and Society*, Vol. 35 No. 1, pp. 47-62.

Global Reporting Initiative (GRI) (2013) G4 sustainability reporting guidelines– Reporting principles and standard disclosure. https://www.globalreporting.org/resourcelibrary/GRIG4-Part1-Reporting-Principles-andStandard -Disclosures.pdf.

GRI, United Nations and WBCSD (2017) SDG Compass. The guide for business action on the SDGs. https://sdgcompass.org. Accessed 15 December 2017.

Hawken P., Lovins A., Lovins L.H. (1999), *Natural capitalism: creating the next industrial revolution*, Little, Brown, Boston, MA.

Hopwood, A.G. (2009), "Accounting and the environment, *Accounting Organizations and Society*", Vol. 34 No. 3-4, pp. 433-439.

Hull C., Rothenberg, S. (2008), "Firm performance: the interactions of corporate social performance with innovation and industry differentiation", *Strategic Management Journal*, Vol. 29 No.7, pp. 781-789.

Iberdrola (2017), Integrated Report, https://www.iberdrola.com/shareholders-investors/annual-reports. Accessed 15 December 2017.

International Integrated Reporting Council (IIRC) (2013) Consultation draft of the international IR framework. http://www.theiirc.org/wp-content/uploads/Consultation-Draft/Consultation-Draft-of-theInternationalIRFramework.pdf.

Jaffe, A., Peterson, S., Portney, P, Stavins, R. (1995), "Environmental regulation and the competitiveness of US manufacturing: what does the evidence tell us?", *Journal of Econic Literature,* Vol. 33 No.1, pp. 132-163.

Joseph, G. (2012), "Ambiguous but tethered: an accounting basis for sustainability reporting", *Critical Perspective on Accounting*, Vol. 23, pp. 93-106.

Miles, M. and Covin, J. (2000), "Environmental marketing: a source of reputational, competitive and financial advantage", *Journal of Business Ethics*, Vol. 23 No. 3, pp. 299-311.

Molina-Azorín, J.F., Claver-Cortés, E., López-Gamero, M.D., Tarí, J.J. (2009), "Green management and financial performance: a literature review", *Management Decision*, Vol. 47 No.7, pp. 1080-1100.

Orlitzky, M., Schmidt, F.L., Rynes, S.L. (2003), "Corporate social and financial performance: a meta- analysis", *Organization Studies*, Vol. 24 No. 3, pp. 403-441.

Pache, A.C., Santos, F. (2011), "Inside the hybrid organization-an organizational level view of responses to conflicting institutional", ESSEC Working Paper 11001.http://www.essec.edu/faculty/showDeclFileRes.do?declId1/49761&key1/4__workpaper.

Porter, M.E., Kramer M.R. (2011), "Creating shared value", *Harvard Business Review*, January-February pp. 1-17.

PWC (2015), Make it your business: Engaging with the Sustainable Development Goals, https://www.pwc.com/gx/en/sustainability/SDG /SDG%20Research_FINAL.pdf. Accessed 27 January 2018.

Sachs, J.D. (2012), "From Millennium Development Goals to Sustainable Development Goals, *Lancet*", 379 pp. 2206-2211.

Schaltegger, S., Etxeberria, I. and Ortas, E. (2017), "Innovating Corporate Accounting and Reporting for Sustainability – Attributes and Challenges", *Sustainable Development*, 25 (1) pp.113-122.

United Nation UN (2010), United Nations Millennium Declaration – General Assembly Resolution A/RES/55/2.

World Commission on Environment and Development (WCED) (1987) Our common future. Oxford University Press, Oxford.

Werbach, A. (2009), *Strategy for sustainability: a business manifesto*, Harvard Business, Boston, MA.

Chapter 4

SUSTAINABLE DEVELOPMENT GOALS AND INTEGRATED THINKING: INTEGRATING SUSTAINABILITY INITIATIVES WITH LONG TERM VALUE CREATION

by *Maria Federica Izzo*

4.1. Introduction

Integrated Thinking and Reporting, as the current frontier of corporate reporting that intends to communicate value creation over time, was introduced and discussed in Chapter 2, while Chapter 3 presented Sustainable Development Goals, a set of goals to end poverty, protect the planet and ensure prosperity for all as part of a new sustainable development agenda.

By drawing upon the elements discussed previously, in this chapter we intend to focus on the possible (and virtuous) interplay between SDGs and integrated thinking.

Sustainable Development Goals represent an enormous challenge for the future of the planet, but achieving these outcomes requires an urgent response from business. In this sense, organisations should shift from a business-centred perspective mainly based on financial capital towards a more integrated value creation approach. Affirming that organisations now welcome and consider SDGs in their business and policies is not sufficient at all. It means nothing if companies do not find a way to effectively integrate SDGs into their business model, strategy and decision-making process.

Recent examples of business engagement with innovation and risk management in response to sustainability challenges are the Integrated Reporting Initiative that advocates integrated sustainability and financial reporting, Action 2020 by the World Business Council for Sustainable Development and the initiative Risky Business which assesses the economic risks of climate change in the United States (Haier *et al.*, 2015).

Along this line, there are two main opportunities brought out by IR in developing and delivering SDGs:

• IR can be used to embed the SDGs in organisations' thinking and reporting, enabling, in this way, their focus on sustainable development.
• IR can be used to demonstrate the impact of a company's value creation process toward sustainable development. IR, in other words, leads to greater transparency and completeness of the outcomes for sustainable development.

The possible advantages of this practice are many. Aligning business approaches to the SDGs with Integrated Reporting can redirect investment flows to maximize value creation and enhance knowledge of the impact of business activities on sustainable development. It can assist organisations in reducing risk, identifying opportunities and delivering long-term, innovative solutions and technologies for addressing sustainable development (Adams, 2017).

Clearly, this is not an easy task as the success of the integration between SDGs and IR is all about trade-offs. As addressed by Gray (2010, p. 57) "any foreseeable sustainable state will be the result of interactions between organisations, individuals, societies and states", but there is something more. The interaction between organisations and societies is anything but simple. SDGs are interdependent goals that can, in certain cases, be divergent and the organisations' value creation process comprises a vast and heterogeneous set of activities and requires the involvement of capitals that very often encompasses trade-offs.

The global effect of these interactions is complexity.

Integrated thinking and reporting can play an active role in rationalizing this process, delivering SDGs and addressing the challenges that managing complexity imposes.

By relying on the previous premises, this chapter aims to explore the intertwining and potentially fruitful relationships between IR and SDGs. The aim is to identify the challenges and opportunities arising from an integrated approach towards sustainable development and the role of this approach in enabling organisations to contribute to a challenge that concerns the entire planet. In this sense, particular attention will be given to the perspective of organisations as active players of this journey, in the attempt to overcome the more commercial and financial needs of the business, in the interest of present and future generations.

In order to achieve the goal described above, this chapter relies upon the analysis of the link between SDGs and integrated thinking (Section 2), with the intention of offering new insights into the value creation process and the trade-offs between SDGs (sometimes independent and potentially conflicting) and capitals, as defined by the <IR> Framework (IIRC, 2013). Next, the ways in which integrated thinking can support organisations in addressing SDGs are explored (Section 3).

In this context, some examples of companies, which have linked their contribution to the SDGs with outcomes for the capitals presented in the <IR> Framework, are presented and discussed in Section 4.

The main messages of this chapter are then summarised in Section 5.

4.2. Toward long-term value creation processes: the link between SDGs and Integrated Thinking

Integrated Reporting is a process that results in communicating value creation over time, through the annual integrated report. It is based on integrated thinking, which is the active consideration by an organisation of the relationships between its various units and the capitals (financial, manufactured, intellectual, human, social and relationship, and natural) that the organisation uses or affects.

According to the IIRC (2013), "the cycle of integrated thinking and reporting, resulting in efficient and productive capital allocation, will act as a force for financial stability and sustainability". This is immediately applicable at a corporate level, but if we embrace a wider perspective, it is possible to assume that integrated thinking is also consistent with the agenda for sustainable development.

As emphasised by Adams (2017), the International <IR> Framework (IIRC, 2013) can be used to aid the understanding of the relationship between sustainable development and value creation.

There are at least two elements that clearly support this statement:

• Value is not created by or within an organisation alone. It is influenced by the external environment; it is impacted by the relationships with stakeholders, and it depends on various resources.

• The external environment of any organisation is affected by issues related to SDGs. The relationships with stakeholders are influenced by the organisations' disclosure and impact. The sustainable development issues pose limitations on the availability of capitals on which organisations rely and, at the same time, the transformation of the capitals often relates to one or more SDGs.

The two dimensions of integrated thinking and sustainable development, then, are strictly dependent and interconnected. The <IR> Framework requires organisations to identify significant factors affecting the external environment and the organisation's response (par. 4.5) and the mate-riality determination process (par 3.18) involves activities, such as: identify-ing relevant matters based on their ability to affect value creation; evaluat-ing the importance of relevant matters in terms of their known or potential effect on value creation; prioritizing the matters based on their relative im-portance and determining the information to disclose about material matters.

In other words, organisations must be aware that the value created in the long term depends on the achievement of one or more of the SDGs, such as, responsible consumption and production, decent work and eco-nomic growth, or climate action.

In light of the above, organisations should reassess their strategy and business model in order to consider risk and opportunities arising from sustainable development issues together with their impact on capitals and their contribution to the SDGs' targets.

This alignment with SDGs can lead to greater transparency of the out-comes of corporate activities on sustainable development and can permit a comparison among organisations.

The next figure depicts how the value creation process, at the level of the organisation, – as presented on page 13 of the <IR> Framework – can be re-formulated by incorporating the SDGs' issues and opportunities to-ward the creation of value over time. This is because the value creation process set out in the Framework can facilitate a focus on sustainable de-velopment, showing the possible link between the value that organisations can create for themselves and the value that they can create for others.

Exhibit 4.1. Linking IR value creation processes and SDGs.

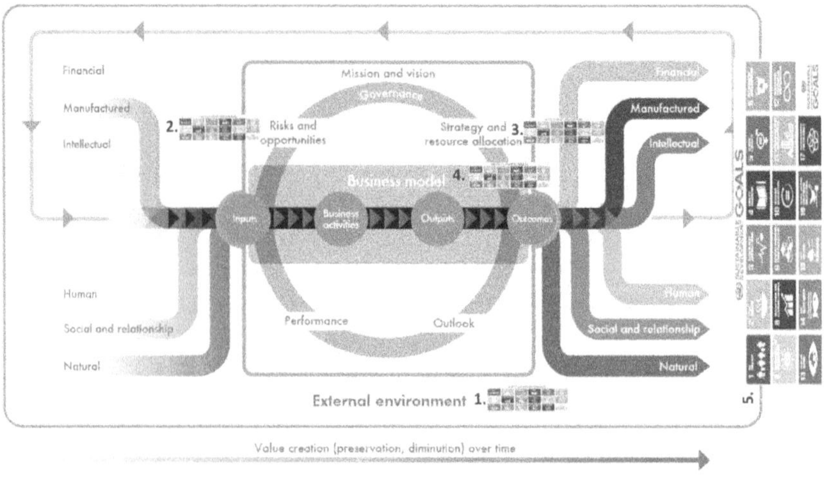

According to the IIRC (2013), integrated thinking leads to integrated decision making and actions that consider the creation of value over the short, medium and long term.

Considers the connectivity and interdependencies between a range of factors that affect an organisation's ability to create value over time, including:

• the capitals that the organisation uses or affects, and the critical interdependencies, including trade-offs, between them;

• the capacity of the organisation to respond to key stakeholders' legitimate needs and interests;

• how the organisation tailors its business model and strategy to respond to its external environment and the risks and opportunities it faces;

• the organisation's activities, performance (financial and other) and outcomes in terms of capitals – in the past, present and future.

All of these factors are related or impacted by SDGs and integrated thinking can be used to embed them in organisations' strategy as well as in the reporting processes.

The outcomes and contributions of companies to the SDGs, in fact, are becoming an important value driver for investors worldwide. During a single decade, defining the value of a company has shifted from a pure tangible issue to an integrated perspective. Integrating the SDGs in the core business and reporting cycle can enable companies to focus on creating visible (and measurable) shared value (Porter and Kramer, 2011). This value can be derived by using a number of measurements and reporting approaches. Integrate Reporting fits perfectly into this scenario.

An integrated report, as illustrated in the previous chapters, is built around seven elements:

• organisational overview and external environment,
• governance,
• risk and opportunities,
• strategy and resource allocation,
• performance,
• outlook, and
• business model.

By linking these elements (or some of them) to SDGs, an organisation can construct the story about its value creation process. In particular, as shown in exhibit 4.3, SDGs are inevitably connected with external environment and risks and opportunities and they can (should?) impact and be integrated in the strategy and business model.

The goals addressed by the U.N. are inextricably linked with the environment in which organisations compete (point 1 in Exhibit 4.3). Considering the characteristics of the external environment, therefore, requires organisations to address SDGs and the sustainable development issues that are relevant to the organisation's ability to create value. Ignoring them will correspond to undermining the opportunities for growth and success and the actual implementation of organisations' strategy.

Additionally, given the nature of the issues considered, scanning the external environment will permit organisations to identify short, medium and long-term risks and opportunities associated with social and environmental issues (point 2 in Exhibit 4.3) which need to be considered when developing strategy (point 3 in Exhibit 4.3) and evolving the business model (point 4 in Exhibit 4.3).

Achieving value requires an understanding of stakeholder needs and some of them, i.e. investors, may require that companies prioritize specific SDGs. Integrated reporting, in this sense, may help organisations to provide information that will support the reallocation of capital required to achieve the SDGs. Sustainability reporting and information about an organisation's contribution to the SDGs, in fact, have gained traction among pension funds and long-term investors, as they recognized a potential risk-reduction effect from these policies and practices.

One of the main advantages of addressing SDGs, in this sense, is allowing companies to anticipate stakeholder expectations and future policy directions at regional, national and international levels.

In relation to the effects, international business has a significant impact on sustainable development issues (and sustainable development goals) and this is easily understandable by adopting a multi-capital approach. In this sense, recognizing that value creation is not possible by simply accumulating financial capital means that value is created or destroyed through different capitals. These capitals (point 5 in Exhibit 5.4), then, will be defined and impacted by integrated thinking, and will, potentially, contribute to SDGs.

When companies (or their business models) transform capitals, they influence one or more SDGs and, at the same time, the strategy undertaken can contribute to the value creation process in a win-win situation.

Aligning the SDGs to the value creation process (see Exhibit 4.4), then, should encompass a series of steps (proposed by Adams, 2017) – in a continuous and iterative cycle – in which organisations:

- *Enlarge their approach to the external environment, explicitly consid-*

ering risks and opportunities associated with sustainable development. In this way, they are identifying external factors that can both influence or be influenced by organisations' activities. From a practical point of view, in fact, the implementation of this environmental scanning will vary considerably in relation to the organisation's business or sector, to the geographical area in which it operates and to the capitals employed and transformed.

• *Define and prioritize sustainable development issues, considering their specific characteristics.* This will lead organisations to identify the elements which present material risks and opportunities for their journey toward value. In this phase, stakeholder engagement can play a strategic role in defining these material issues, since they are fundamental for the value creation process.

• *Incorporate the material issues previously identified in the strategy definition process.* If steps 1 and 2 are properly developed, then value can be created only by addressing these issues through the organisation's strategy and aligning them with the business model.

• *Embed all the considerations mentioned above into the process of integrated thinking, facing the trade-offs that exist among different SDGs and different capitals.* Thanks to this approach, organisations will properly consider the connectivity and interdependencies between a range of factors that affect an organisation's ability to create value over time (IIRC, 2013).

• *Inform organisation members and stakeholders in a clear way about their contribution to SDGs through the integrated report.* These results should be presented alongside the information about capitals. Providers of financial capital need information about the externalities of organisations' activities, and the increasing, decreasing and transformation of capitals, in order to assess their effects and allocate resources accordingly. As illustrated, in fact, organisations are called upon to contribute to sustainable development processes and are pushed to incorporate SDGs into their strategy and to communicate the results and outcomes generated to stakeholders. In the integrated report, it is possible and reasonable to depict the links and the relationships between the capitals (used and/or affected) and the SDGs, through the value creation process.

Exhibit 4.2. SDGs and the value creation process.

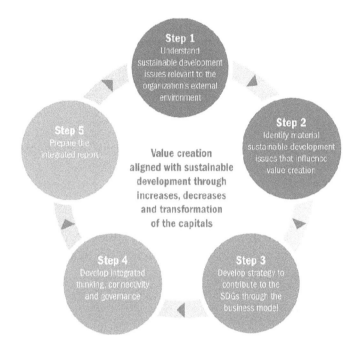

Source: Adams, 2017, p. 22.

The approach to SDGs and value, as described above, is meant to contribute to the sustainable development process through integrated thinking and reporting practices. From this point of view, organisations are required to implement integration, define ad hoc strategies and adopt business models that capture social, environmental and financial dimensions and outcomes as well as their intertwining relationships.

4.3. Delivering SDGs through Integrated Thinking

In the last year, as noted in the previous chapters, there has been a strong increase in the number of sustainability reports and sustainable disclosure in general, which is in line with the increased stakeholder demand for non-financial information. An increasing number of companies adopted external reporting standards, such as the Global Reporting Initiative and Integrated Reporting, while at the same time they are improving their internal management accounting systems for non-financial information. In addition, the European Union Directive 2014/95/EU has obliged companies with more than 500 employees, 20 million euros in assets, and 40 million euros in revenues to disclose relevant and useful information in their management report about their policies, main risks and outcomes relating to environmental matters; social and employee aspects; respect for human rights; anticorruption and bribery issues; and gender diversity in the board of directors.

This trend calls for the definition and implementation of more effective methods of disclosure that organisations can use to report their progress on the SDGs in order to continue their journey toward sustainable development and inform their stakeholders. Organisations need to be transparent about the impact they are having by focusing on stakeholders and by maintaining a relationship of trust with them, therefore, encouraging sustainable policies that help to ensure the stability of the business model in the medium and long term.

The Sustainable Development Goals present an opportunity for the private sector to align corporate strategy with countries' development priorities, playing a key role in sustainable development, and adopting shared value strategies as well as changing its behaviour and approach by focusing on long-term and sustainable performances. To be able to deliver long-term value, organisations need a holistic strategy and an integrated approach to business and value.

In this framework, integrated thinking plays a key role in managing impact more holistically, allowing organisations:

• to build connectivity across departments and, in this way, having more impact in creating sustainable value;
• to improve the ability of evaluating risks and opportunities more effectively, leading to a robust decision-making process;
• to improve their dialogue with stakeholders.

At the higher level, integrated thinking should assist organisations in properly integrating SDGs into their strategy and business model, facilitating a process of understanding how key sustainability drivers and initiatives contribute to achieving business and financial strategies and goals. Consequently, the challenges and opportunities that arise from an integrated approach towards sustainability lead companies to make SDGs a central element of the process of planning, budgeting, and performance measurement, and include sustainability targets and objectives in performance appraisal.

At the same time, referring to an organisation's governance structure, integrated thinking shall provide insights on how ensure that the SDGs and their connection with the organisation's strategy are understood cross-functionally in the business organisation.

Moreover, integrated thinking can support organisations in integrating the management of sustainable development issues into everyday business decision making and, then, in properly communicating, through a meaningful and effective way, the results obtained. Since effective reporting is significantly more than just a simple a piece of communication to key stakeholders, it creates trust and supports value creation – and can be a powerful tool to stimulate internal changes and decision making through integrated performance management.

At the same time, reporting on SDGs can protect (or create) the organisation's licence to operate and integrated thinking can help organisations in mapping and measuring its impact, implementing its sustainable initiatives and creating a complete dialogue with stakeholders.

From a practical point of view, integrated thinking can support companies in addressing and delivering SDGs by facilitating a number of processes that permit the alignment of strategy and business model with sustainable development issues. In order to effectively manage these processes, a company should:

1. secure the understanding, interest, and commitment of high profile organisation leaders who are willing to champion the adoption of the SDGs;

2. map and prioritize the SDGs relevant to the organisation's business model and incorporate the SDGs into company strategy;

3. design a system of alignment between capitals and SDGs and define their reciprocal impacts within the business model;

4. create a cross-functional work group to ensure engagement, diversity, and inclusiveness while the concept of integration is being applied to planning, measurement, and reporting;

5. clarify the difference between performing sustainability and sustainable performance(s) early in the process, and bring the finance sector onboard, together with other organisational functions;

6. focus on the purpose of the business and on the multiple objectives to be achieved, considering the various stakeholders that engage within the value chain;

7. understand the financial, operating and ESG objectives as well as the expected targets that are linked into the organisation's strategic plan;

8. identify the resources, the activities, the drivers, and the stakeholders that are involved in the development and execution of the business model;

9. recognize the trade-offs, interests and risks that characterize the value creation process – especially across and within the capitals and the SDGs;

10. share the achievements of the SDGs in order to regain society's trust and secure the license to operate by working with governments, consumers, workers and civil society.

4.4. How companies make SDGs happen through Integrated Reporting: cases and best practices

As discussed above, according to the IR Framework, value is derived from a number of interactions, activities, and relationships that could affect the increase, decrease or transformation of the various kinds of capitals of an organisation. Consequently, organisations and their business models generate outcomes (internal vs. external and positive vs. negative) that affect and are affecting, in turn, the external environment. Organisations are, therefore, a part of a more interconnected environment and they can strongly influence it. This is even more evident in relation to SDGs.

Currently, organisations are being called on to assess and manage their impact on sustainable development, and so the aim of this section is to identify some best practices in companies that are implementing and communicating this integrated approach toward SDGs and IR beyond its mere rhetoric.

The following paragraphs present a collection of cases that describe how a number of companies, which are active in different sectors, are approaching SDGs through integrated thinking and reporting. These case studies focus on the following companies: City Development Limited, a real estate company based in Singapore and operating worldwide; Itaú Unibanco Holdings SA, a Brazilian publicly quoted bank, which is currently the biggest Latin American bank by assets and market capitalization; Cbus Superannuation Fund, one of Australia's largest public offer industry superannuation funds.

4.4.1. City Developments Limited: an integrated strategy for value creation

City Developments Limited (CDL) is a Singapore-listed international real estate operating company with a global presence spanning 97 locations in 26 countries. As one of Singapore's largest companies by market capitalisation, its investing portfolio comprises residences, offices, hotels, serviced apartments, integrated developments and shopping malls totalling over 18 million square feet of floor area globally.

CDL has hotel assets in one of the world's largest hotel groups and its London-listed subsidiary, Millennium & Copthorne Hotels plc (M&C), has over 130 hotels globally, many in key gateway cities.

In addition to hotels, the CDL Group currently owns and manages a strong portfolio of residential and investment properties across Asia, Europe, the Middle East, North America and New Zealand/Australia.

In 2016, the company earned 3.9 billion Singapore dollars (2.4 billion euros), with an increase of 9% as compared to the previous fiscal year and their net profit was 763 million Singapore dollars (468 million euros).

The mission statement of the company is as follows: "As a trusted property pioneer and a global hotelier, City Developments Limited builds value everywhere we go". As a consequence, CDL is committed to "build sustainable profitability while conserving the environment and build bonds with the community by supporting worthy causes".

Sustainability has been historically a top priority of the company, which proudly informs in its 2016 Integrated Report that it has 22 years of sustainability integration into business strategy and operations and it is listed on 12 leading sustainability indices including FTSE4Good Index Series, MSCI Global Sustainability Indexes and Dow Jones Sustainability Indices (City Developments Limited, 2017: 2).

From 2008, a company-wide Sustainability Committee was set up to drive sustainability across all corporate and operational units of CDL. Led by the Chief Sustainability Officer with guidance from the Senior Management, the committee initiates, drives, and monitors various aspects of sustainability practices, aiming at ensuring effective integration of environmental, social and governance (ESG) initiatives into business operations and corporate objectives. Above this committee sits a Board Sustainability Committee that assumes an advisory role for CDL's sustainability strategy. This Board-level committee meets at least once a year to review CDL's ESG performance and initiatives.

Initially called the CSR and Corporate Governance Committee, the Board Sustainability Committee was renamed in November 2016 to better reflect the Board's role in advancing sustainability within the organisation.

Exhibit 4.3. CDL Sustainability Committee Structure.

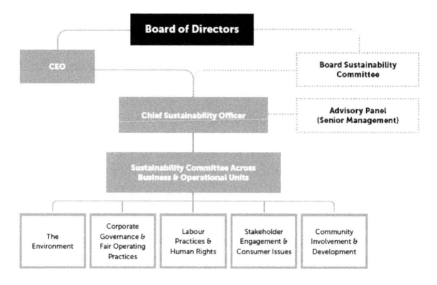

Aligned with ISO 26000: Guidance on social responsibility

Source: CDL, 2017, p. 11.

In the last few years, CDL launched a series of projects that have supported a massive process of integration and alignment with sustainable development.

The company has centred Environmental, Social and Governance (ESG) issues on its value creation process, actively engaging with existing shareholders and potential investors to communicate its business case for ESG integration. This is because CDL's Board considers ESG integration as being essential to a company's long-term success and economic value. For example, as suggested by the Executive Chairman "there has been progressively more evidence that investors are placing greater importance on such [ESG] data, believing in a causal link between good ESG practices and the long-term success and economic value of a company, beyond just pursuing financial returns. Furthermore, research has now shown that investors are actively incorporating such data into investment decisions, reinforcing the business case for sustainability. Businesses must adapt to the increasing importance of sustainability, capitalise on such opportunities and unlock the potential of integrating sustainability into their operations".

In light of the above, from 2015, CDL has established strong links between remuneration – both at executive and employee levels – and corporate sustainability performance. ESG indicators that are aligned with global standards, such as, for example, ISO 26000, ISO 140001 and GRI Standards have been incorporated in the individual goal setting of all employees, including senior management. In this way, CDL recognises that integration between appropriate ESG issues, company goals and incentive schemes is a strategic factor in creating long lasting value and promoting accountability in CSR practices.

In 2015, the company was the first private developer in Singapore to adopt the International Integrated Reporting Council's Integrated Reporting Framework for sustainability reporting. In 2016, it started to align its material ESG issues with UN SDGs and finally, in 2017 introduced a new sustainability blueprint that traces the company direction to 2030.

Labelled as "CDL Future Value 2030", the blueprint opens with a letter written by City Development Limited's CEO, who addresses some of the topics included within the document.

In this letter, the CEO describes value creation within the company, strongly affirming that ESG integration is now essential to the company's long-term success and economic value. The CEO's letter conveys the role of six capitals – financial, organisational, natural, manufactured, human as well as social and relationship – in creating tangible value for business, stakeholders, community and the environment. Referring to the journey ahead, he states: "Under our new CDL Future Value 2030 blueprint, we will actively track and review our sustainability performance against the ESG goals and targets established to support CDL's growth while complementing the UN SDGs".

This blueprint was developed with three main intentions:

- reinforce the CDL's long established sustainability strategy and best practices in creating value for business, investors, stakeholders, community and the planet;
- set out clear directions and Environmental, Social and Governance (ESG) goals material to CDL's business and stakeholders;
- maintain CDL's position as a sustainable leader in the real estate management and development sector.

The choice of 2030 as the reference point of this challenging process is motivated by different situations that make this year a sustainability milestone for both the planet and the company.

Besides being the target year for the United Nations (UN) Sustainable Development Goals, 2030 is also fundamental for the Paris Agreement, and, finally, for the building industry it represents the focal point for the Net Zero Agenda by the World Green Building Council and for Singapore to green 80% of its buildings based on the Green Building Masterplan.

In addressing CDL Future Value 2030, the company decided to reassess the ESG issues that were considered material for its business, through a review of the materiality assessment completed in November 2014. Thanks to an online survey managed by an independent consultant, seven stakeholder groups[1] were asked to rank a list of 22 ESG issues, and provide feedback on any additional issues they assumed to be important to CDL business.

The stakeholder engagement was strong and their response rate quite high (75%), outlining the relevance of ESG issues for the business success.

Starting from these results, CDL applied the methodology of AA1000's materiality process to map the 22 ESG issues onto a matrix, reflecting their importance to external and internal stakeholders, in order to rank the top 10 most critical ESG issues. The latter were finally reviewed and endorsed by the Board of Directors in February 2017.

What is particularly relevant here, is that the company, starting from these results, decided to assess the material ESG issues against the UN's 2030 Agenda for Sustainable Development by aligning them with nine relevant SDGs, ultimately finding that all the top ten material issues have an impact (or multiple impacts) on SDGs, especially SDG 8, 9, 7, 12 and 13.

Exhibit 4.4. CDL Top 10 material issues.

Top 10 Material Issues		
Legal Compliance		SDG: 16
Anti-corruption and Anti-fraud		SDG: 16
Product Quality and Responsibility		SDG: 7,9,11,12,15
Employee Health and Safety		SDG: 8
Customer/Public Health and Safety		SDG: 8
Economic Contribution to Society		SDG: 8,9,11,12,13
Supplier Health and Safety		SDG: 8
Customer and Tenant Engagement		SDG: 7,13
Energy Efficiency		SDG: 7,9,12,13
Environmental Impact Assessment and Mitigation		SDG: 9,15

Source: Our elaboration from CDL, 2017, p.18.

---

[1] In line with Freeman's well-known definition (1984, p. 46) – "any group or individual who can affect or is affected by the achievement of the organisation's objectives" –, CDL defines its stakeholder as "groups whom our business has a significant impact on, and those with a vested interest in our operations". The relevant stakeholders identified are Employees; Customers; Builders and Suppliers; Investors; Government and Regulators; Media and Community.

In the same document, CDL goes even further, aligning its capitals (manufactured; social and relationship; natural; organisational and human) with the SDGs already defined as relevant and material for its stakeholders.

This effort is particularly relevant for at least two reasons.

Firstly, it demonstrates the relevance of the topic and the related debate about SDGs for successful companies, such as CDL. Secondly, it introduces a new step in disclosing, integrating capitals, past performances and specific targets defined by the single organisation and global goals identified by the United Nations.

Interestingly enough, the main challenges of sustainable development, both at global and organisation levels, seem to be fully integrated, as presented in Exhibit 4.5.

As emphasised in the previous chapter, for CDL and for any organisations on the planet, the SDG challenge can represent an opportunity to review its (their) approach to business and to identify opportunities to strengthen the integration of sustainable development into the business agenda and processes.

On this point, CDL, both in its Integrated Sustainability Report and Annual Report, recognises that disconnection (or a lack of integration) between sustainability and risk management can lead to strategic and operational risks as well as missed opportunities for growth.

Interestingly enough, among these risks CDL lists the following: climate change risks, health and safety risks, people risks, product risks, raw materials supply risks, regulatory risks and water risks.

Instead, the opportunities linked to ESG are: demographic shifts, low carbon economy, responsible investment and green financing, and sharing economy.

It is interesting to note that the majority of risks and advantages screened by the company are strictly linked to SDGs, meaning that companies that decide to correctly address SDGs will have the opportunity to minimize risks and take advantage of making SDGs happen.

Exhibit 4.5. CDL Integrated strategy for value creation.

CDL's Capital	Performance Highlights in 2016	CDL Future Value 2030: ESG Goals and Targets (Effective from 2017)	Supporting Nine Relevant SDGs
Manufactured Capital	• 87 Green Mark certified developments and office interiors • More than 70% of CDL's portfolio of Green Mark certified developments and properties are rated Green Mark Gold^plus and Platinum – beyond the mandatory Green Mark certification level	**Goal 1: Building Sustainable Cities and Communities** • To achieve Green Mark certification for 80% of CDL owned and/or managed buildings	SDG 11: Sustainable Cities and Communities
Social and Relationship Capital	• Over 95% of our existing tenants have signed on to the CDL Green Lease Partnership Programme	• To maintain 100% tenant participation in CDL Green Lease Partnership Programme	
	• Invested $2.25 million in an R&D collaboration with National University of Singapore (NUS) to catalyse innovations in climate-resilient and smart building technologies through NUS-CDL Smart Green Home and Tropical Technologies Laboratory (T^2 Lab)	• To double our commitment to adopt innovations and technology for green buildings	SDG 9: Resilient and Innovative Infrastructure
	• Announced the launch of the Singapore Sustainability Academy – a hub for capacity building, advocacy and stakeholder engagement for sustainable development, in partnership with the Sustainable Energy Association of Singapore	• To double resources devoted to advocacy of sustainability practices, stakeholder engagement and capacity building	SDG 17: Partnership for Sustainable Development
Natural Capital	• Reduced carbon emissions intensity by 16% from 2007 levels • First property developer in Singapore to achieve ISO 14064 assurance for Greenhouse Gases (GHG) emissions disclosure	**Goal 2: Reducing Environmental Impact** • To achieve the science-based target of reducing carbon emissions* intensity by 38% from 2007 levels	SDG 13: Urgent Action to Combat Climate Change
	• Reduced energy use intensity by 25% from 2007 levels • Reduced water use intensity by 15% from 2007 levels	• To reduce the usage intensity of energy and water by 25% from 2007 levels	SDG 7: Affordable and Clean Energy

	• Established 2016 baseline for new waste disposal target
	  – 13,523 tonnes of construction waste
	  – 4,283 tonnes of general, non-hazardous waste from commercial buildings
		• To reduce total waste disposed by 50% from 2016 levels	SDG 12: Responsible Consumption and Production

	• Almost 100% of consultants and main builders of CDL developments have obtained both ISO14001 and OHSAS18001 certifications	• To ensure 100% of appointed suppliers are certified by recognised environmental standards	
	• At least 80% of the Singapore Sustainability Academy was built with Cross Laminated Timber and Glued Laminated Timber, which are harvested from sustainably managed forests and verified by the Nature's Barcode™ system	• To ensure that 50% of our construction materials are derived from recycled content, low-carbon sources or certified by recognised environmental organisations	SDG 15: Biodiversity and Resource Conservation
Organisational Capital	• Zero corruption and fraud incidents across CDL's core operations in Singapore	**Goal 3: Ensuring Fair, Safe and Inclusive Workplace** • To maintain Zero corruption and fraud incidents across CDL's core operations	SDG 16: Peace, Justice and Strong Institutions
Human Capital	• Zero fatality across CDL's operations and direct suppliers in Singapore	• To maintain Zero fatality across CDL's operations and direct suppliers in Singapore	SDG 8: Decent Work and Economic Growth
	• Zero occupational diseases across CDL's operations and direct suppliers in Singapore	• To maintain Zero occupational diseases across CDL's operations and direct suppliers in Singapore	
	• Accident Frequency Rate (AFR)* of 5.7 at corporate office • AFR of 0.53 at construction sites • Zero AFR at managed properties	• To maintain Zero AFR at CDL corporate office • To maintain AFR of one or less for direct suppliers at construction sites and managed properties	

Source: CDL, 2017, pp. 14-15.

Referring to the risks identified by CDL, it is quite simple to directly relate some of them to one or more SDGs.

Climate change risks, that include risks driven by changes in regulations, physical climate parameters and other climate-related developments, can be controlled by addressing SDG 13 (climate action).

Health and safety risks, influenced by an unsafe work environment, are linked to SDG 3 (good health and well-being) and SDG 8 (decent work and economic growth).

In facing product risks and raw materials supply risks, CDL addresses Goal 9 (industry, innovation and infrastructure) as well as Goal 11 (sustainable cities and communities). As a big player in the real estate market, as a matter of fact, it makes it a priority to deliver innovative green and safe designs with high standards of workmanship and functionality. At the same time, it recognises that the stability and the sustainability of the supply and production of materials have a direct impact on CDL's core business operations.

Finally, water risks are obviously linked to Goal 6 (clean water and sanitation). To ensure a reduction in the use of potable water in construction, CDL closely monitors water consumption with set targets in place.

Similarly, the opportunities identified by CDL correspond to potential benefits that companies can obtain by developing and delivering solutions for the achievement of SDGs.

The demographic shift and the new needs of an older world's population may correspond to a future business opportunity (see Chapter 3) and CDL (as many other companies) can capitalise on the benefits connected to Goal 11 (sustainable cities and communities), enlarging its offer and its product portfolio.

At the same time, its long-lasting history as an eco-developer can help CDL to leverage on Goal 7 (affordable and clean energy) and as a first mover in the field, to take advantage of the green growth economy. As reported in the Integrated Sustainability Report, by 2020, the global low-carbon and resource efficient industry is projected to reach US $ 2.2 trillion.

4.4.2. Itaú Unibanco Holdings SA

Itaú Unibanco Holdings SA (IUH) is a publicly listed financial holding company operating in the banking industry and providing a range of financial products and services to individual and corporate clients in Brazil and abroad. It is the second Brazilian bank with a market share of 16%, immediately after Banco do Brasil that controls the 18% of the Brazilian banking industry.

The company provides various types of banking activities through its commercial, investment, real estate loan, finance and investment credit, and lease portfolios, including foreign exchange operations. Through its subsidiaries, IUH is also engaged in other activities, with a focus on insurance, private pension plans, capitalization, securities brokerage and administration of credit cards, consortia, and investment funds and managed portfolios.

The company has over 5,100 branches and client service branches, and operates through three segments: Retail Banking, Wholesale Banking, and Activities with the Market and Corporation.

The company's Retail Banking segment offers banking products and services to a diversified client base of account holders and non-account holders, individuals and companies. The Retail Banking segment includes retail clients, high net worth clients and the corporate segment (very small and small companies).

The company's Wholesale Banking segment offers products and services to middle-market companies, high net worth clients (private banking) and institutional clients.

Finally, the company's Activities with the Market and Corporation segment mainly manages the financial results associated with capital surplus, subordinated debt and net debt of tax credits and debits.

The IUH Integrated Report 2016 opens with a message from the Chairman of the Board and CEO who states the following: "Over the past few years, we have been able to generate consistent results that are in line with our strategies. To us, to create value means to carry out business in a way that is sustainable and relevant for the society in which we are inserted" (IUH, 2017, p. 3).

In this sense, the company vision is particularly relevant, as presented in the Sustainability section of the report: Itaú Unibanco Holdings wants "to be the leading bank in sustainable performance and customer satisfaction".

IUH has supported the integration of sustainability into its business at length by addressing the incorporation of environmental and social issues into the daily activities and processes in all areas of the group.

Interestingly, the company governance structure identifies different layers of sustainability focus, distinguishing among board, executive, officers and operational levels.

The Board of Directors is in charge of the long-term strategic sustainability decisions that are discussed during the Strategy Committee meeting, which is composed of members of the Board of Directors and of the Executive Committee.

At the executive level, the members of the Executive Committee sit in the Superior Ethics and Sustainability Committee, which is responsible for integrating ethics and sustainability practices to promote the dissemination of topics to the business management, organisational culture and strategy.

Exhibit 4.6. Sustainability Governance at IUH.

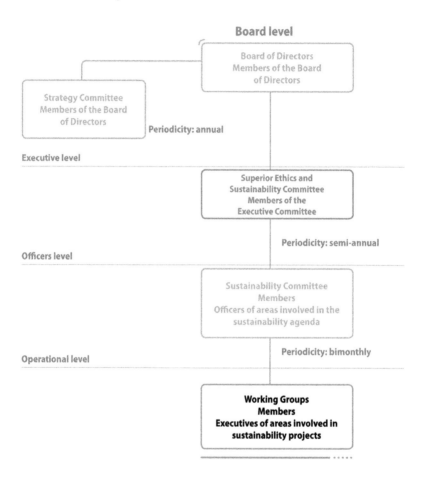

Source: IUH, 2017, p. 52.

Then, at the officers level, the Sustainability Committee addresses the main sustainability issues from the bank's governance and respective working groups. In 2016, for example, it discussed the revision of Sustainability Governance to strengthen and combine the sustainability strategy with the activities developed by the group. With the aim of integrating the requests, skills and knowledge of the entire company, this committee is composed of representatives from different areas, including: Legal, Personnel Management Department, Internal Controls, Compliance, Governmental and Institutional Relations, Corporate Communication, Investors Relations, Credit Risk and Modeling and Sustainability.

Finally, at the operational level, the company set up working groups to enhance the execution of the sustainability strategy and integrate sustainable initiatives into business areas. These groups are responsible for managing projects and other initiatives relating to sustainability issues.

Sustainability is a company priority and IUH defines its vision by affirming that creating value means to obtain sustainable results in an ethical and responsible way that meets the needs of the company's stakeholders. This value creation process (the company explicitly refers to a shared value creation process) depends on the capitals that the company uses and affects.

Specifically, IUH presents a brief description of the capitals that are most relevant to its business model:

• Financial capital is composed of the financial resources available and allocated to the businesses, obtained in the form of products and services provided to clients, such as: loan operations, financial investments, deposits and funding, investments and operations with insurance, pension and capitalization.

• Social and relationship capital mainly refers to relationships with clients, stockholders, investors, suppliers, regulatory agencies, government and society.

• These relationships are ethical and transparent, and the related capital also includes the ability to share value with stakeholders as the company wants to enhance both individual and collective well-being.

• Human capital relies on employees and their skills and experiences, as well as their motivations to innovate and develop better products and services, in an ethical and responsible way.

• Intellectual capital is composed of the reputation obtained, in the time, by the brand, by technical knowledge and intellectual property and by the ability to develop new technologies, products and services for the sustainability of the business.

• Manufactured capital is built on equipment and physical installations, such as branches, ATMs, applications and systems that are used by the organisation in the provision of products and services. It is fundamental for the day by day relationships between the company and its clients.

• Natural capital, finally, refers to renewable and non-renewable environmental resources, consumed or affected by the businesses, for the prosperity of the organisation.

According to the IUH Integrated Report 2017, in 2016 the value added reached R$70.0 billion (17.5 billion euros) and mainly referred to financial capital (31.7%), social and relationship capital (35.2%) and human capital (29%). The rest was distributed as follows: intellectual capital 2.4%, manufactured 1.1% and natural capital 0.6%.

IUH's approach to capitals is enriched by (a) the identification of themes that are material to its capability to create shared value and (b) the effort to link these themes both to the most affected stakeholder and the impacted Sustainable Development Goals.

As previously discussed, thanks to integrated thinking promoted by the IR Framework, organisations are stimulated to focus on the connectivity and interdependencies among a range of factors that have a material effect on their ability to create value over time. In this sense, Exhibit 4.7 clearly defines the global approach of the company to creating value by identifying 4 pillars: material themes, capitals, stakeholders and SDGs.

Determining material themes is crucial to guide decision making, since it provides a broader vision of the risks and opportunities inherent in the business and connects strategies to the varying external interests.

The inputs (or capitals) used by the company are the basis of its business model. Due to its activity, IUH primarily affects and is affected by financial capital and social and relationship capital, but all the other capitals are fundamental for its success.

In this sense, the value creation process can be significant only if stakeholders are correctly engaged and assumed to be a part of the prioritization stage, which is required to define material themes. In IUH, the determination of the key stakeholders is carried out according to what is called the Sustainable Performance Spiral, which defines Society, Stockholder, Clients and Employees as the basis for the virtuous cycle of sustainable development (IUH, 2017, p. 52).

Finally, the company believes that impactful contributions to the SDGs can be obtained through its own business and value chain, mainly in relation to SDG 8 (decent work and economic growth) since the banking system plays a key role in boosting economic growth and has become part of the everyday life of millions of people; and also, SDG 9 (industry innovation and infrastructure); 16 (peace, justice and strong institutions) and 17 (partnership for the goals).

Exhibit 4.7. From material themes to SDGs.

Material themes	Capital most exposed to the theme					Most affected stakeholders				Sustainable Development Goals (SDGs)
Credit and insolvency						+				-
Risk and capital management						+				1, 8, 9, 10, 13, 15
Efficiency						+				9
Diversification of revenue						+				-
Attraction, retention and development						+				4, 5, 8
Forecast of scenarios						+				-
Client satisfaction						+				-
Ethics and transparency						+				16, 17
Information security						+				16
Corporate governance						+				-
Innovation						+				-
Corporate citizenship						+				1, 4, 8, 9, 10, 11, 16, 17
Financial education and inclusion						+				1, 8, 9, 10, 12, 17
Management of suppliers and supply chain						+				1, 5, 8, 9, 12, 16, 17
Compensation and incentives						+				5, 8
Information technology						+				-
Brand and reputation						+				16
International operations						+				-
Combat of corruption and illegal activities						+				16, 17
Diversity, equity and inclusion						+				5, 8, 10, 16, 17
Occupational health, safety and well-being						+				3, 8, 16
Eco-efficiency and environmental management						+				3, 6, 7, 8, 9, 11, 12, 13, 14, 15

Source: IUH, 2017, p. 57.

In this scenario, the report suggests how IUH can play an active role in addressing sustainable development by balancing financial goals and sustainable performance at a global level. This has led the company to measure itself against the SDGs and communicate its involvement in finding concrete solutions to providing excellent service to its clients and, at the same time, moving toward the achievement of the SDGs.

By taking a look at the previous exhibit, it is possible to make some interesting conclusions.

As a major operator in the banking sector, "risk and capital management" represents one of the most relevant themes prioritized by stakeholders and refers to all of the six capitals identified in the IR Framework. It is considered to be an essential instrument for optimizing the resources employed, assisting in selecting business opportunities and maximizing value creation to stakeholders as, primarily, clients and stockholders.

At the same time, this theme can impact and be impacted by society and it is considered to be crucial in contributing to sustainable development. Financial institutions, in fact, play a wide range of roles in society by safeguarding savings, facilitating efficient allocation of capital to support economic growth, providing broad access to financial services and products. Consequently, according to the IUH Integrated Report 2017, risk and capital management can influence six out of seventeen SDGs. Interestingly enough, it could even be related to climate change (SDG 13) and life on land (SDG 15), as it impacts and is impacted by environmental and social risk. The company, in fact, is aware of the potential financial losses and reputational damages that are linked to these kinds of risks and so it is continuously implementing a risk mitigating strategy.

By analysing Exhibit 4.7, "Management of suppliers and supply chain" appears to be one of the themes that is most affected by the stakeholder 'Society' and that, at the same time, refers to a higher number of SDGs. It is related to the promotion of sustainable practices along the supply chain and for this reason it can produce a strong impact on the value chain of the company and on the produced externalities. The Management of suppliers and supply chain entails a big portion of the company activity and value creation process. It covers a wide range of segments – such as telecommunications, call centres, cash and valuables deliveries, market research, furnishings, electricity and training programs – and the relationships with these partners is inspired by transparency and sustainability principles.

IUH declares to have approximately 9,000 partners that provide goods or services to its business. This partnership is made through a formal contract process whose objective is to minimize possible financial, reputational, operational and legal impacts during the provision of the service or upon the termination of the contract. They also undertake efforts to improve sustainable practices, as well as conformity with the legislation and ethical principles that must govern business relationships.

IUH's cooperation model has been finalized to maximize its positive impact on society and reinforce local development and sustainable performance.

In both the Annual Report and Integrated Report, the company presents the results of a study, developed by a specialized consulting firm, which intends to measure the socio-economic contribution of Itaú Unibanco operations and impacts generated by ten different credit-related products offered to clients. This contribution entails three distinct kinds of impacts attributable to company activity: direct impact, indirect impact and induced impact.

Referring to suppliers (through an indirect effect) the study calculates that the company generated an impact on the Brazilian GDP of R$100 billion (24.7 billion euros), contributing to maintaining the equivalent of 2,463 jobs.

Finally, while implicitly recalling SDG 13, the IUH Integrated Report 2017 includes a section dedicated to "Ecoefficiency and climate change", in which Itaú Unibanco Holding defines climate change as one of the key challenges of the present and the future.

As a financial institution, IUH recognizes itself as a change agent, playing a key role in mitigating these risks and supporting the transition to a low-carbon economy.

Obviously, the company recognizes that by comparing itself to a company operating in the industrial sector, its own potential impact on climate change is lower; nevertheless, its activity does have an impact on the environment though water and electric power consumption and waste. The shortage of natural resources and climate risks, in fact, bring dire consequences to society and the economy.

The company's commitment to promoting this awareness lies in incorporating climate change-related variables into its operations and business areas (credit, insurance and investments) by managing risks through the experience of its environmental and social risk analysis team. Therefore, it is developing solutions that adequately respond to GHG emission reduction targets and adapting its operations to the best industry practices to mitigate the effects of climate changes on its activities. At the same time, it is integrating climate variables into its business, managing risks and seeking alternatives to increase its resilience, ensuring the longevity of business and contribution to society.

Examples of this effort are the three IUH's administrative buildings that hold environmental certifications. In 2016, Edifício Faria Lima 3500 was awarded LEED – Operation and Maintenance's GOLD seal that represents one more important environmental certification in addition to the certification LEED – New Construction obtained for the CTMM technological centre. In the same year the company renewed the ISO 14001 certification for Tatuapé Administrative Center.

4.4.3. Cbus Superannuation Fund

The Construction and Building Unions Superannuation (Cbus) Fund is one of the largest Australian public offer Industry Superannuation funds. It is a privately owned corporate pension plan sponsor, also providing retirement planning and superannuation services to both employers and individuals. Interestingly, Australia's 1.3 trillion euros of tax-advantaged retirement savings is among the world's largest after the U.S., U.K., Japan and Canada.

The Cbus Industry Superannuation Fund was founded in 1984 and is based in Victoria, Australia. It now has over 755,000 members (workers and retirees, their families and employers), with 325 staff across three states.

The Cbus Fund directly and wholly controls Cbus Property, the subsidiary responsible for the development and management of Cbus' direct property investments. From 2006 to 30 June 2017, Cbus Property has returned 15.95% on average each year to its members, investing over 2 billion Australian Dollars (1.3 billion euros) in building projects across Australia and creating over 75,000 direct jobs[2].

The Cbus's mission is "to maximise returns to members, and not profit to shareholders". In doing so, they "actively support and contribute to a sustainable and growing industry and are committed to inclusion, transparency and accountability in the way they work".

The Cbus Annual Integrated Report 2017 defines its priorities immediately on page 1, acknowledging the company's role in helping the Australian Government to fulfil its responsibilities of achieving the SDGs. Differently from the Annual Integrated Report 2016, the company, systematically used the SDG icons throughout the report to show how its work contributes to the achievement of these goals.

Specifically, they are seen in the Message from the CEO and define sustainable development as one outcome of its business model. A complete section is dedicated to the SDGs, labelled "Pension funds, Cbus and the

---

[2] Estimation based on inductions for completed and committed developments. Source: https://www.cbussuper.com.au/about-us/cbus-property, accessed 15 January 2018.

Sustainable Development Goals", positioning the development of its approach to the SDGs (see Exhibit 4.8) into its responsible investment journey that started in 2001, and then graphically identifying which of the SDGs it contributes to for each of its key activities, which are identified as contributing to value creation.

In 2016, instead, the discussion about SDGs was simply sketched, introducing six of the seventeen SDGs that they had prioritized and affirming that the achievement of the Sustainable Development Goals set by the United Nations would have a positive impact on long-term investment returns, moreover, defining the 2016/2017 priorities in this way:

- renewal and implementation of ESG policy including adoption of the UN Sustainable Development Goals;
- deeper engagement and long-term investment in companies that take their sustainability practices seriously;
- investment in the built environment – property and infrastructure.

Cbus commenced its engagement and focus on Environmental, Social and Governance (ESG) issues in 2001 by joining national and global initiatives to find out more about issues that were relevant to long-term investing, advocating for change and commencing engagement strategies.

In 2002 it began incorporating ESG provisions in fund manager and investment manager agreements, clearly demonstrating its effort to align these topics with strategy and its approach to investment. This awareness culminated in the ESG manager being appointed to the Investment Team in 2009. Meanwhile, in 2006 it signed the Principles of Responsible Investment (PRI) and in 2009 it endorsed the Carbon Disclosure Project (CDP). In 2010 it issued its first stand-alone ESG Policy and pursued sustainability, leading a massive process of exclusions from its investment portfolio of companies involved in tobacco products and the manufacture of controversial weapons. This was because Cbus' focus is to actively engage with the companies they invest in around their ESG practices, aiming them to continue to provide strong, sustainable returns to members over the long term. This policy appears immediately consistent with SDG 17 – Global partnership for sustainable development. Clearly, it reveals the sustainable position of Cbus, resulting in taking the view that addressing environmental, social and governance issues is critical to long-term stability and success in business and investing.

Exhibit 4.8. Cbus' responsible investment journey.

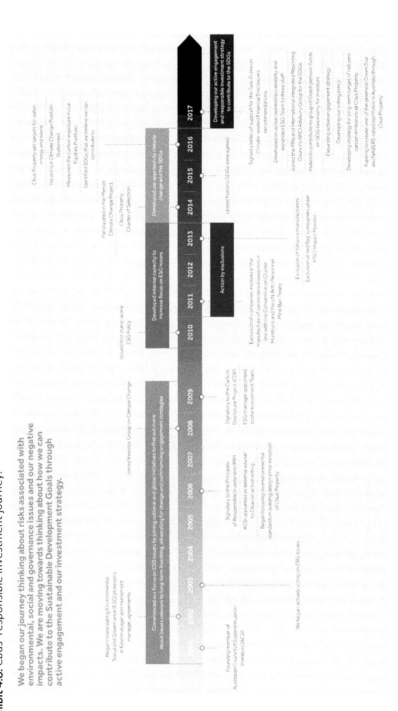

We began our journey thinking about risks associated with environmental, social and governance issues and our negative impacts. We are moving towards thinking about how we can contribute to the Sustainable Development Goals through active engagement and our investment strategy.

Source: Cbus, 2017, p. 15.

Since 2013, Cbus has been a part of the Global Pension Network for Integrated Reporting, which aims to ensure that its reporting framework articulates strategy and drives performance. It has recently introduced the GRI G4 framework to report its sustainability impacts and performance. Finally, in 2017 it joined the International Integrated Reporting Council's (IIRC) Advisory Group for the SDGs.

By expanding an active engagement strategy by developing projects for the long-term target of net zero carbon emissions at Cbus Property, stimulating economic growth, and enhancing the lives of people around the world, the company believes that contributions that have a clear impact on the SDGs will be made through its own business and its value chain.

Cbus underlines the opportunities and risks associated with SDGs, together with the interconnections among them and the multiple effects triggered by its activities. The company explicitly recognizes that its strategic activities may contribute to more than one SDG, including those not listed and analysed in the report. However, its discussion focuses on the six SDGs that it identified in 2015/16 and that the company assumes are directly relevant to the competitiveness and value of its investments.

The identification process of these six SDGs considered a set of strategic and operating elements, such as: investment decisions, business partnerships, responsibilities as a property developer through Cbus Property, their role as an employer and relationships with stakeholders, policy makers and domestic and global influencers.

Interestingly enough, in line with the trade-offs we discussed in the first part of this chapter, the SDGs that the company believes it can make the most significant contribution to are: SDG 5 – Gender equality; SDG 8 – Sustainable economic growth; SDG 9 – Build resilient infrastructure; SDG 11 – Make cities safe, resilient and sustainable; SDG 13 – Climate Change and SDG 17 – Global partnerships for sustainable development.

SDGs 8, 9, 11 and 13 are particularly relevant to the company's strategy due to its business model and primary activity. As a long-term investor and through Cbus Property, SDG 9 and 11 have a particular impact from its innovative approaches to design and construction, as well as its contribution to the competitiveness and long-term sustainability of Australian and overseas infrastructure.

In relation to the main topics of this chapter, Cbus acknowledges that its contributions to SDGs also represent outcomes for the multiple capitals of integrated reporting and contribute to value created for its members. As depicted in Exhibit 4.8, the final step of its business model corresponds to the outcomes generated, which refer to the six capitals of the IR Framework. In line with the main activities of the fund, the purpose of addressing sustainable development and minimising environmental impacts is directly related to natural capital (graphically indicated with a sun on a blue background), social and relationship capital (in the Exhibit, a globe) and manufactured capital (two stylised buildings).

Then, throughout the report various capital icons are pictured when the company uses them in the value creation process. Examples of these representations are related to company strategy toward 2020; the ambitious project of expanding Cbus' digital capability or its focus on the partnership and distribution model, to name a few. For each of these activities the Integrated Report shows the SDG (or SDGs) impacted and the capital (or capitals) used, transformed or generated.

Illustrating its strategy, Cbus declares its effort in creating value for members through investing their superannuation contributions, returning all profits to members and providing solutions to help them achieve a dignified retirement.

Specifically, the company identifies the four main pillars of its strategy on the basis of different targets that are related to: member, employer, retirement and investments. These strategic pillars are then explored in relation to the key programs the company intends to develop and, finally, the corresponding capital for each target is identified. For example, one of the main targets of Cbus for 2020, referring to member, is to have more than 70% of active members at an adequate retirement savings level. The key "Program of work" that supports this strategy relies on the enhancement of the member experience, thanks to solutions, such as:

• extend the advice model capacity to deliver the transition and retirement capability and improve retention;
• enhance the insurance claims experience;
• implement the personalised member portal;
• increase engagement with sponsoring organisations to drive member growth.

Exhibit 4.9. Cbus's outcomes.

Source: Cbus, 2017, p. 5.

In addressing these challenges, the company must leverage its intellectual capital that should enable technology and business architecture to deliver an integrated digital capability. Intellectual capital is also recalled (both as input and as outcome), referring to Cbus' "Partnership and distribution model", together with Financial, Human and Social and Relationship capital.

As previously mentioned, Cbus' Industry Partnership program, designed to facilitate the creation of productive partnerships between Cbus and key industry stakeholder organisations, is particularly relevant in relation to its impact on SDG 17 – Global partnership for sustainable development. As a major operator in the industry fund sector, partnerships are a key aspect of Cbus' business model as the long-term strength in performance of industry funds can be attributed to the industrial ecosystem in which they operate. In this sense, Cbus firstly evaluates its industry partnerships using a model that measures the advocacy benefit delivered by Cbus' industry partner and then, it defines partnership agreements that are delivered through commercial contracts meeting the following key deliverables (assumed to be relevant and strategic):

- opportunities to retain and grow the fund's member base;
- direct advertising and brand benefits;
- advocacy building engagements;
- activities that promote members and their employer's engagement with the fund;
- opportunities to progress Cbus' broader strategic imperatives.

Addressing SDG 17, Cbus recognizes that its "partnerships create the most value where Cbus' and its partner's interests intersect. The greater that alignment is, then the greater the opportunity is for the partnership to create value for both organisations" and, we can add, to the global system.

Also, thanks to this program, ultimately, Cbus demonstrates how the capitals used are integrated in its strategy by identifying the sustainable development goals connected to it, and presenting its Integrated Report as a key governance initiative for communicating value to stakeholders.

4.5. Summary and conclusions

In this chapter we have highlighted the need for a concrete joint organisation effort to embed sustainable development issues in their decision-making processes, strategies, business model and even in the process of planning, budgeting, and performance measurement. The first attempts to include sustainability targets and objectives in performance appraisal are valuable, but the journey ahead is challenging.

On these issues, companies in business and finance need to move further and faster. Here, governments have a clear role in setting the right incentives for good practices that are consistent with SDG goals and targets, and disincentivizing unsustainable systems and practices.

We have emphasised the role that organisations play in promoting and realizing SDGs and, at the same time, the interconnections between SDGs and integrated thinking along the path of the long-term value creation process. Nevertheless, the synergies and tensions between these dimensions deserve further consideration. Both of them are moving toward similar objectives: to define risks, prioritize activities and develop a clear strategy that, in a conscious way, can internalize sustainable development's risks and opportunities.

At the same time, integrated thinking can support and facilitate the implementation of SDGs in a number of ways. By transforming capitals to create value both for itself and for others, a company can make a significant and material contribution to SDGs. Integrating SDGs into the business model and strategy can offer useful insights to investors in addressing their concerns, their risk evaluation and in raising their awareness of the importance of sustainable development in the long-term value creation process.

Based on integrated thinking, the integrated report should report on how the business model delivers positive and negative outcomes for multiple capitals and how this contributes to the SDGs.

Finally, the cases presented in this chapter demonstrate the possibility to make the alignment between SDGs and the six capitals introduced by IIRC Framework real. Linking an organisation's contribution to the SDGs with outcomes for the six capitals can demonstrate how such integration creates value for both organisations and for the society as well as the planet. An integrated report could be a useful tool through which to discuss the challenges and opportunities for creating value (and sustainable development) in the short, medium and long term.

The interrelationship between integrated thinking and SDGs is currently a lively and engaging theme, worthy of further exploration, both theoretically and practically, around the globe. In this sense, the evidence presented in the business case study discussions clearly requires further analysis since the SDGs were only agreed on at the end of 2015. Therefore, while the practice is still emerging, it is easy to anticipate increasing innovation in integrating thinking (and reporting) for the SDGs.

4.6. References

Adams, C. (2017), The Sustainable Development Goals, integrated thinking and the Integrated report, http://integratedreporting.org/resource/sdgs-integrated-thinking-and-the-integrated-report/. Accessed 15 January 2008.

Cbus (2017), Annual Integrated Report 2017, https://www.cbussuper.com.au/about-us/annual-report. Accessed 27 January 2008.

Cbus, (2016), Annual Integrated Report 2016,https://www.cbussuper.com.au/content/dam/cbus/files/governance/reporting/Annual-Integrated-Report-2016.pdf. Accessed 27 January 2008.

CDL (2017), CDL Future Value 2030. Integrated Sustainability Report, https://www.cdlsustainability.com/cdl-future-value-2030/. Accessed 27 January 2008.

Gray, R. (2010), "Is accounting for sustainability actually accounting for sustainability…and how would we know? An exploration of narratives of organisations and the planet", *Accounting, Organisations and Society*, Vol. 35 No. 1, pp. 47-62.

Hajer, M., Nilsson, M., Raworth, K., Bakker, P., Berkhout, F., de Boer, Y., Rockström, J., Ludwig, K. 1 and Kok, M. (2015), "Beyond Cockpit-ism: Four Insights to Enhance the Transformative Potential of the Sustainable Development Goals", *Sustainability*, Vo. 7 No. 2, pp. 1651-1660.

International Integrated Reporting Council. International <IR> Framework. (2013). http://www.theiirc.org/wp-content/uploads/Consultation-Draft/Consultation-Draft-of-the-InternationalIRFramework.pdf. Accessed 15 January 2008.

IUH (2016), Integrated Report 2016. http://www.itau.com.br/annual-report Accessed 27 January 2008.

Porter, M.E., Kramer, M.R. (2011), "Creating shared value", *Harvard Business Review*, January-February: pp. 1-17.

Chapter 5
CONCLUSIONS

by *Fabrizio Granà* and *Maria Federica Izzo* [1]

SUMMARY: 5.1. The momentum of Sustainable Developments Goals. – 5.2. The role of business in fostering SDGs within organization strategies. – 5.3. Opportunities for integrating SDGs within business strategies: the role of CEOs. – 5.4. Summary and further thoughts. – 5.5. References.

5.1. The momentum of Sustainable Development Goals

Sustainable Development Goals are a relatively new phenomenon in the world of business and have gained significant momentum in the last three years, also because the world has been experiencing unprecedented economic growth and benefiting from technological and digital developments that have strongly improved possibilities and conditions of millions of people around the world. Despite these successes, we are today witnessing an intensifying climate change, biodiversity and ecosystem damage, unprecedented depletion of natural resources and a strong rise in inequalities within populations. In this scenario, societies, global institutions, businesses and citizens must play (and are encouraged to play) a key role in leading a change towards sustainable development.

Sustainable Development Goals (SDGs) represent a powerful instrument for organizations for moving toward a novel sustainable growth model that aims to reduce exposure to risks, produces benefits for both organizations and the economic system and opens new opportunities in terms of innovation, reputation and efficiency gains. In this context, organizations have to face the challenge of turning policies into action and dare taking a more consistent approach to sustainable issues by conducting robust impact assessment and reporting their performances. According to PwC (2015), an organization's approach and reporting on SDGs often depends on the industry characteristics, competitor policies and the expectations of heterogeneous stakeholders (see Exhibit 5.1).

In addition, the analysis of the UN Global Compact (2017), on the re-

---

[1] Although this chapter is the result of a joint effort, section 5.1 can be assigned to Maria Federica Izzo. The following sections (5.2, 5.3, 5.4) can be assigned to Fabrizio Granà.

porting process of its members, reveals significant progress in engagement and reporting practices on SDGs. According to their data:

- 75% of companies have actions in place to address the Sustainable Development Goals;
- Sustainable Development strategies and policies are monitored at CEO level in 69% of businesses;
- 55% of companies align their core business strategy with one or more relevant UN goals/issues,
- 70% of companies are reporting publicly about their progress with sustainable development and 55% of businesses note that reporting helps them in embedding sustainability into the business.

Exhibit 5.1. Top business impacts by industry.

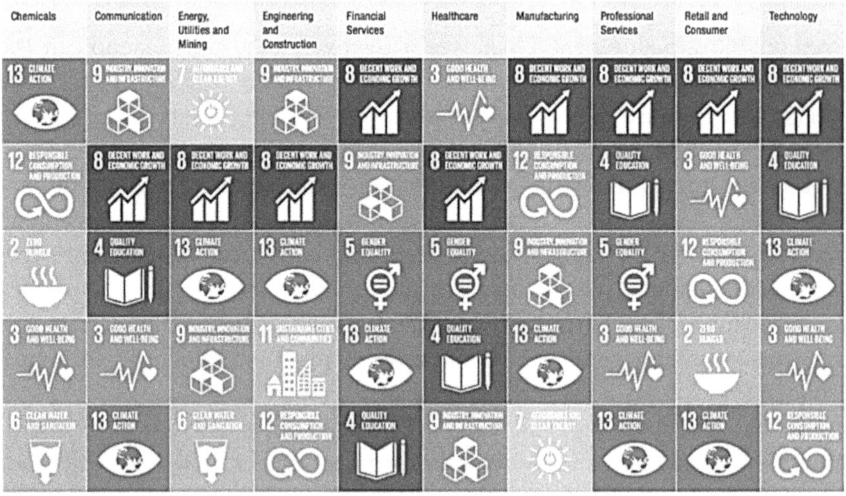

Source: PwC, 2015, p. 11.

According to the case studies illustrated in this study, we can maintain that the success of SDGs is achievable within organizations through: the integration and alignment of SDGs with strategies and business models and correct disclosure that communicates responsible corporate practices, performances and outcomes. In particular, we recognize the necessity to shape and transform organizations' strategies towards a much greater alignment between their purpose and sustainable development goals.

In this regard, we maintain that Integrated Thinking and reporting may contribute toward the achievement of SDGs by bringing organizations' top managers, particularly, the Chief Executive Officers (CEOs) on board through these initiatives. Business leaders have a key role in striking out in new directions and redesigning organizations' strategies to embrace more sustainable and inclusive economic models (WBCSD, 2017). Moreover, Integrated Thinking contributes to the management of any negative impacts on their traditional activities, identifying opportunities and innovative solutions for addressing sustainable development.

In this concluding chapter, we illustrate the main benefits of integrating SDGs within organization strategies. In particular, Section 5.2 illustrates the role of business in fostering SDGs within organizations' strategies. Section 5.3 focuses on the role of CEOs in integrating SDGs within organizations. Finally, some conclusive comments are provided in Section 5.4.

5.2. The role of business in fostering SDGs within organization strategies

> 'Too many companies today put resources into social development initiatives that are worthy on their face, while ignoring serious negative impacts on people in their own operations and value chains. So, they end up giving with one hand while taking away – or enabling others to do so – with the other. This is not a pathway to sustainable development.'
>
> John G. Ruggie, former UN Secretary-General's Special Representative on Business and Human Rights (Ruggie, 2016)

Today's economic model is considered to be the major cause of a list of environmental and social disruptions that may negatively affect future growth prospects. At the same time, these issues may turn out to be an increasing business cost, making the world "a less viable place in which to conduct business" (WBCSD, 2017a, p.12). For these reasons, organizations are required to understand and assess the positive or negative impacts of their traditional activities, determining whether they offer a help or a hindrance to the achievement of Sustainable Development Goals (PwC, 2017). However, while there have been promising and progressive efforts from organizations and their leaders to rethink their value creation process in order to meet the requests of a growing number of external stakeholders, they are still confined within indefensible and ludicrous short-term profit walls, giving marginal consideration to sustainable development (OXFAM, 2017).

As many businesses are constrained by the need to maximize shareholder value, there can be no real step by step change in their positive contributions to society without a change in the way that the overall purpose of business is defined. Business structures can play a critical role in determining the trade-off between a focus on profit maximization and sustainable development objectives. They may empower stakeholders' requests over key decisions and resolve trade-offs between multiple stakeholder interests (OXFAM, 2017).

Focusing on short term objectives and growth can be counterproductive in the long term and may hinder the ability of other organizations to pursue SDGs.

Although SDGs have been often considered as being spread across the environmental, social, economic and governance dimensions (see Exhibit 5.2), organizations are tempted to prioritise them based on their potential economic impact and still face constraints in integrating them within their strategies.

Exhibit 5.2. Classifying SDGs according to social, environmental, economic and governance dimensions.

Source: BSCD, 2017a, p. 20.

At the moment, organizations tend to 'cherry pick' the SDGs they want to focus on and ignore others that don't meet their corporate priorities or comfort zones. According to a survey published by PwC in 2017, just 1% of companies they surveyed is planning to assess their impact on all 17 SDGs. While 34% said they were planning to assess some SDGs that are relevant to their business (PwC, 2017, p. 12). Although prioritising one or two SDGs is easier to achieve for medium and long-term targets that are suitable for internal strategies, from an honesty and transparency perspective this approach would be seen by governments and broader stakeholders as a way to appeal to the media, without driving business performance more closely to SDGs (PwC, 2017).

For the goal of the SDGs to be realized, businesses will need to engage in more than a few cosmetic "window dressing" changes. The application of SDGs within organizations' decision-making process offers a new framework for economic growth and requires a systemic change, which implies coordinated action in order to achieve progress[2]. In this regard, the SDGs challenge current business models going beyond the responsibility of individual organizations.

The ambition of the SDGs is not only to challenge traditional organizational initiatives towards the achievement of broader social, environmental, economic and governance issues, but requires a global movement that challenges the existence of entire industries (BSDC, 2017, p. 22). According to the BSDC (2017) there are strong links between the environmental and economic clusters. For example, "effective action on climate change will be essential to achieving the objectives of strong economic growth and ending poverty, while access to affordable energy will help reduce inequality and support sustainable industrialisation in the developing world. At the same time, major investments in infrastructure and innovation will be needed to meet the environmental goals set in the SDGs. Links between the social and environmental clusters are also critically important: sustainable management of land and water ecosystems will help improve agricultural productivity and eliminate hunger and malnutrition, while climate action, better housing and less polluted cities will have widespread benefits on health and well-being" (p. 23).

---

[2] On this point, the world leader in communications technology and services, Ericsson, represents a very interesting exception. The company, in fact, assigns each of their executive leadership team members to be a champion of one of the SDGs and ensure that they carry forward opportunities to engage on that SDG.

Exhibit 5.3. Connecting SDGS and their social, environmental and economic effects.

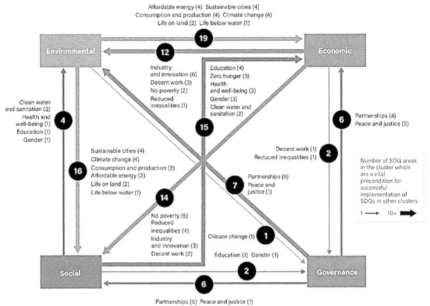

Source: BSCD, 2017a, p. 23.

But, how can organizations shift from using a narrow business case approach to aligning their core activities with broader societal values and interests? How could organizations integrate sustainable development into their strategies?

In one of its Discussion Papers, the Oxford Committee for Famine Relief (OXFAM) proposes at least three pathways toward more meaningful business engagement in the SDGs (OXFAM, 2017, p. 3).

First it asks companies to *Prioritize an understanding of impact.* Organizations' priorities and initiatives should be reviewed to determine their impact (positive and negative) on a variety of stakeholders. Strengthening engagement relations with organizations' stakeholders would improve accountability and transparency of information in the eyes of investors, consumers and governments while aligning companies with the ambition of the SDGs to 'leave no one behind'. Second companies should *align core business strategies with the SDGs.* If organizations are aimed at pursuing SDGs, they must broaden and deepen their partnerships, aligning their core business practices and strategies toward sustainable development (OXFAM, 2017). Third organizations should *work toward systemic change.* Organizations together with regulators, governments, investors and civil society as a whole should work together to align organizations' agendas for sustainable development. By setting rules (regulators), incentives or punishments (governments), rewarding more meaningful SDG engagement (investors) and exposing irresponsible behaviour (civil society), organizations may be brought toward the enactment and achievement of SDGs, improving social cohesiveness and ambitions toward sustainable development; promoting a new mindset of what meaningful engagement in the SDGs should look like, supporting leaders in challenging the feasibility of adopting sustainable business strategies.

5.3. Opportunities for integrating SDGs within business strategies: the role of CEOs

The integration of SDGs within organizations' business models represents both a substantial opportunity and an important challenge: an opportunity since it brings the benefits of additional investments, skills and innovation from the business sector, and a challenge in that it gives unprecedented power and expectations to organizations as fundamental actors toward sustainable development.

According to the BSDC (2017a, p.6), the private sector will be crucial to delivering the SDGs, and it stands to benefit from a potential US $ 12 trillion worth of business opportunities, which could create almost 380 million jobs by 2030 – more than 10 percent of the forecasted labour force in 2030.

Some of the opportunities that the integration of SDGs may bring have been clustered and classified in four industry systems (food and agriculture; cities; energy and materials; and health and well-being) (BSDC, 2017b, p. 13).

However, the geographic distribution of these SDG opportunities may have more or less effect depending on the industry system taken into account. For instance, in the case of cities, improving the efficiency of buildings is most critical in the developing world. The value of opportunities involving energy and materials is distributed quite evenly. However, extractive activities and opportunities take place primarily in the developing world, while the benefits from the production and marketing of extractive goods are likely to emerge faster in developed markets. In the case of food and agriculture, there are substantial opportunities in developing countries in Africa, Latin America and India, however, their productivity is quite low. Health and well-being opportunities are concentrated in developing countries, where access is currently low (BSDC, 2017, p.13).

Substantial investment will be needed to capture the SDGs' opportunities. The Business and Sustainable Development Commission estimates that the total annual investment required for all 60 opportunities, across the four industries, is around US$4 trillion. Even though the supply of capital is expected to be adequate to achieve these business opportunities, it will be challenging to ensure that the investment reaches the regions where it is most needed, especially in the developing countries (BSDC, 2017b).

Exhibit 5.4. Opportunities for business in four main industries.

	Food and agriculture	Cities	Energy and materials	Health and well-being
1	Reducing food waste in value chain	Affordable housing	Circular models - automotive	Risk pooling
2	Forest ecosystem services	Energy efficiency - buildings	Expansion of renewables	Remote patient monitoring
3	Low-income food markets	Electric and hybrid vehicles	Circular models - appliances	Telehealth
4	Reducing consumer food waste	Public transport in urban areas	Circular models - electronics	Advanced genomics
5	Product reformulation	Car sharing	Energy efficiency - non-energy intensive industries	Activity services
6	Technology in large-scale farms	Road safety equipment	Energy storage systems	Detection of counterfeit drugs
7	Dietary switch	Autonomous vehicles	Resource recovery	Tobacco control
8	Sustainable aquaculture	Internal combustion engine vehicle fuel efficiency	End-use steel efficiency	Weight management programs
9	Technology in smallholder farms	Building resilient cities	Energy efficiency - energy intensive industries	Better disease management
10	Micro-irrigation	Municipal water leakage	Carbon capture and storage	Electronic medical records
11	Restoring degraded land	Cultural tourism	Energy access	Better maternal and child health
12	Reducing packaging waste	Smart metering	Green chemicals	Healthcare training
13	Cattle intensification	Water and sanitation infrastructure	Additive manufacturing	Low-cost surgery
14	Urban agriculture	Office sharing	Local content in extractives	
15		Timber buildings	Shared infrastructure	
16		Durable and modular buildings	Mine rehabilitation	
17			Grid interconnection	

Source: BSDC, 2017a, p. 13.

While business is not being asked to deliver the SDGs alone, these opportunities cannot be realized without meaningful engagement by business leaders, CEOs and, more generally, organization board members.

According to the Business and Sustainable Development Commission any business leader should inspire aspiration toward SDGs and commitment among managers within organizations by adopting the six main actions (BSDC, 2017b, pp. 15-16):

1) *Build support for Sustainable Development Goals (SDGs) as the right growth strategy within organizations and across the business community*. The more business leaders understand the business case for the SDGs, the faster progress will be toward better business in a better world.

2) *Incorporate the SDGs into the organization strategy*. In particular, by applying SDGs at the strategic level CEOs can create opportunities for businesses to grow in new markets that are more successful and sustainable, marketing products and services that would inspire consumers to make sustainable choices, and using the goals to guide leadership development, women's empowerment at every level, regulatory policy and capital allocation.

3) *Drive the transformation to sustainable markets with sector peers*. CEO's would be required to work in partnership with sector peers and stakeholders to collectively map their actions within the same sustainable competitive field and stabilize societies and market purpose through progress on the SDGs.

4) *Work with policy-makers to pay the true cost of natural and human resources*. In particular, business leaders would be required to keep pace with policy developments, working openly with regulators, business and civil society to shape fiscal and regulatory policies that create a competitive playing field that is more in line with the SDGs.

5) *Push for a financial system oriented towards longer-term sustainable investment.* Because of the world's currently uncertain circumstances, most investors are looking for liquidity and short-term gains. However, business leaders can buck the trend by strengthening the flow of capital into sustainable investments. This approach would positive affect the enhanced value and return on investment of corporate sustainability through partnerships and strengthening corporate relationships with stakeholders.

6) *Rebuilding the Social Contract*. Business leaders can regain society's trust and secure their licenses to operate by working with governments, consumers, workers and civil society by adopting responsible and open policy advocacy.

5.4. Summary and further thoughts

Today, organizations operate in a complex and rapidly changing world that is characterized by a multitude of internal and external drivers, interdependencies and trade-offs that influence the process of decision making and the promises that these decisions entail. Within this context, most organizations strive to balance competitiveness and sustainable development by implementing programs and initiatives of sustainability that intend to achieve specific targets in terms of governance, social, and environmental impact. It is evident that there is still disconnection within organizations regarding their awareness of and plans to act on SDGs. The concepts, elements and principles that characterize the ways in which organizations plan, manage and report their approach to SDGs are currently being questioned, debated, and redesigned throughout the world. This is happening as key notions such as capital(s) employed, value creation and accountability are redefined in practice.

A cultural shift is, however, required to support such a process. A paradigm shift must be rooted in the reorganization of systems, processes and practices, while seeking to meet the Sustainable Development Goals.

In this context, CEOs may have a great opportunity to lead the process of making SDGs happen in practice and connect performance with purpose, providing adequate management accounting and reporting tools to link between multiple "capitals", facilitating engagement across multiple stakeholders. Because of their leading expertise and positioning within organizations, CEOs can contribute significantly to identifying, executing, and monitoring business decisions and strategies for long-term value creation.

In this regard, management accounting and reporting tools such as integrated thinking and reporting offer engagement platforms that provide a set of ad hoc targets and key performance indicators to include the SDGs into organizations' traditional processes, mediating among the different stakeholders who are involved. Integrated thinking and reporting may provide a powerful tool for increasing the internal and external awareness, especially among investors, of the way in which the integrated management of the business is currently practiced towards SDGs. Through integrated thinking and reporting organizations can better represent the way in which sustainability's objectives and multiple perspectives are fully embedded within the company's business model and decision-making processes.

This is obviously the beginning of a journey that we believe will mark a change in the way companies conceive their business models and report on SDGs to enable a more sustainable management and to enhance the achievement of sustainable value creation in the future.

5.5. References

Bekefi, T. and Epstein, M. (2016), 21st Century Sustainability, Strategic Finance, November.

BSDC, Business Sustainable Development Commission (2017a), Better business Better world, http://report.businesscommission.org/reports. Accessed 27 January 2018.

BSDC, Business Sustainable Development Commission (2017b), Valuing the SDG prize. Unlocking business opportunities to accelerate sustainable and Inclusive growth, http://s3.amazonaws.com/aws-bsdc/Valuing-the-SDG-Prize.pdf. Accessed 27 January 2018.

Busco C., Quattrone, P. and Granà, F. (2017), Integrated Thinking: Aligning purpose and the business model to market opportunities and sustainable performance, CIMA Research Report, pp. 1-28.

OXFAM (2017), Raising the BAR. Rethinking the role of business in the Sustainable Development Goals, https://www.oxfam.org/sites/www.oxfam.org/files/dp-raising-the-bar-business-sdgs-130217-en_0.pdf. Accessed 27 January 2018.

Price Waterhouse Cooper – PwC (2015), Make it your business: Engaging with the Sustainable Development Goals, https://www.pwc.com/gx/en/ sustainability/ SDG/SDG%20Research_FINAL.pdf Accessed 27 January 2018.

Ruggie, J.G. (2016), The Sustainable Development Goals and the Guiding Principles. Open letter authored by Shift Chair John Ruggie and sent to the heads of the Global Commission on Business and Sustainable Development. http://www.shiftproject.org/news/john-ruggie-sustainable-development-goals-and-un-guiding-principles. Accessed 17 January 2018.

UN Global Compact (2017), United Nations Global Compact Progress Report. Business solutions to sustainable development, https://www.unglobalcompact.org/library/5431. Accessed 31 January 2018.

WBCSD (2017a), CEO Guide to the Sustainable Development Goals, https://www.wbcsd.org/Overview/Resources/General/CEO-Guide-to-the-SDGs. Accessed 27 January 2018.

WBCSD (2017b), Reporting matters, https://www.wbcsd.org/Projects/Reporting/Reportingmatters/Resources/Reporting-Matters-2017. Accessed 27 January 2018.

For Product Safety Concerns and Information please contact our EU
representative GPSR@taylorandfrancis.com
Taylor & Francis Verlag GmbH, Kaufingerstraße 24, 80331 München, Germany